Beginning Again

Beginning Again

A SPOUSE'S STORY OF LIFE AFTER TRAUMA

Thomas Trezise

UNIVERSITY OF CALIFORNIA PRESS

University of California Press
Oakland, California

Library of Congress Cataloging-in-Publication Data

Names: Trezise, Thomas, 1953- author.
Title: Beginning again: a spouse's story of life after trauma / Thomas Trezise.
Description: Oakland, California University of California Press, [2026]
Identifiers: LCCN 2026017567 (print) | LCCN 2026017568 (ebook) | ISBN 9780520422650 (cloth) | ISBN 9780520422674 (ebook)
Subjects: LCSH: Trezise, Thomas, 1953—Family. | Secondary traumatic stress. | Rape victims—France. | Victims of violent crimes—Family relationships. | Masculinity—Psychological aspects.
Classification: LCC RC552.P67 (print) | LCC RC552.P67 (ebook)
LC record available at https://lccn.loc.gov/2026017567
LC ebook record available at https://lccn.loc.gov/2026017568
Manufactured in the United States of America
GPSR Authorized Representative: Easy Access System Europe, Mustamäe tee 50, 10621 Tallinn, Estonia, gpsr.requests@easproject.com

35 34 33 32 31 30 29 28 27 26
10 9 8 7 6 5 4 3 2 1

For Susan and Gabriel

Contents

1 *Premonition*

I was standing in the sun at a junction of dirt roads. It was July 4th, a holiday back home but just another fine summer day in southern France. At half past noon, a stillness had settled over the countryside in the gathering heat. Even the cicadas were quiet. Occasionally the sound of hammering at a farm down the road, or the distant barking of a dog, or the call of a crow in the tree line would ripple the silence and fade away. Around me was a rolling landscape of interwoven meadows and woods, of checkered greens beneath a bright blue sky. Much like a painting, and just as motionless.

I'd come out to see if I could glimpse her walking toward me in the distance or even pick up the sound of her footsteps. She'd been gone a long time. And this was the middle of nowhere. There were no distractions here to account for her absence as there would have been in a city or town. No shops with enticing window displays, no cafés where you could rest your feet and sip an ice-cold pastis in the shade, no passersby you could strike up a conversation with. This was a remote area we'd never visited before.

I kept thinking about that moment when she headed out of the house in her sweatshirt, jeans, and running shoes. It must have been around 10:30. I was sitting at a table near the door, working with a French colleague on the English translation of a book of his. We'd come to his partner's country place, a forty-minute drive from Grenoble, so I could discuss revisions with him. Going for a walk right then wasn't an option for me, even if I'd been invited. But why, when Susan said she was going alone, did I feel an impulse to hold her back? A sudden unease, inclining me to say something when I didn't even know what it was? After a moment's hesitation, I just smiled at her distractedly as she turned to leave.

It could have been that I was bothered by the feel of this visit, which wasn't shaping up as I'd hoped. After we'd arrived the previous evening, it seemed to me that Philippe, my colleague and former professor, and his partner, Claire, did very little to engage with Susan, the newcomer. They asked few if any questions about her life or career, even though they knew she taught philosophy, like Philippe. And none about us, for that matter, about how we met or our life together. Maybe they were preoccupied. They'd recently learned that their closest friend, Jean-Luc, needed a heart transplant. That would have been enough. Maybe they were tired from a surfeit of guests or simply assumed there'd be time the next day to get better acquainted. Or maybe it was me. Why should I have expected people from very different chapters of my life to hit it off from the start? Especially knowing that Philippe was intensely reserved and that Claire seldom strayed from her own orbit. All the same, I was puzzled and increasingly ill at ease as the evening wore on.

It was no less awkward in the morning, when Claire, who had promised Susan an excursion to the nearest town while we worked, simply left without her. So I couldn't help wondering if the unease I'd experienced as Susan left the house was really an annoyance with our hosts, and if I'd found nothing to say because I could hardly express annoyance with people who'd just welcomed us into their country home. What seemed certain to me was that my French and American worlds weren't meshing very well. But then I wasn't sure this had affected Susan. For all I knew, she'd just felt like going for a walk.

These were idle thoughts, no doubt. But that's just what I was, too—idle, out there at the crossroads, with still no sign of Susan and nothing else to do, with time to ruminate and speculate, time to exaggerate.

Then I recalled an incident from three years before, during a summer we spent in a village in the same region. Early one evening we were driving slowly down the main street on our way to a restaurant when a deafening collision almost lifted our rental car off the ground and left us momentarily stunned. A pedestrian, we thought. We had hit a pedestrian! As I flung the door open and jumped out to see, a young man punched me in the face. Despite my shock, I noticed him reel, glassy-eyed, from his own blow, and suddenly realized that the pedestrian we were worried about was a drunk who'd appeared out of nowhere and hurled himself against the driver's side of the car. The next thing I remembered was Susan shouting "No!" so loud it arrested in midair the counterpunch I'd begun to throw—and at the very same moment the assailant was distracted by a lone passerby running toward him and yelling, "What the hell do you think you're doing?!" When the drunk began to stumble away, the passerby approached us to see if we were okay. But with the village otherwise deserted and the police nowhere in sight, we could only watch as our besotted attacker disappeared around a corner.

All of this happened in less time than it takes to tell. Later, we learned about the rest of the spree he went on before finding his way home, where his father was waiting, also drunk. The two of them, rifles at the ready, held off a whole squad of gendarmes till daybreak.

It's possible this incident was in the back of my mind as I watched Susan leave. Not that it was such a big deal. After all, no one was seriously hurt. We enjoyed the rest of our stay that summer, as far as I remembered, and the rental agency forgave us the dents and scratches. Yet there was something indigestible about that punch in the face, that punch unprovoked and unforeseen. Not to mention the torpedoing that preceded it. Neither of which took place in some tough Parisian neighborhood at two in the morning, but long before sundown in a nice little town called Talloires. What we learned that evening and over the next couple of days exposed an unfamiliar, disturbing profile of rural and small-town France. It was like an image so strikingly imprinted on the retina that you still see it when you look away. It was enough to put me on my guard.

A lot of good that'll do now, I thought. Why didn't I say something? I was still standing at the junction, looking and listening, at a loss for story lines to contain this lengthening delay. Belief in a higher power might have been useful, if only to calm my nerves. Failing that, I could have tried divination, scrutinizing the veins of a dusty leaf by the roadside or coaxing some reassuring numerical symbolism from our birthdates. Anything to pass the time. The fact is I almost yearned for the misgiving I'd sensed as Susan walked out the door, since mere misgiving now looked so comforting in its triviality. But what I really wanted was to fast-forward, to skip the scary stuff. I wanted to cut to a future perfect, secure in the knowledge that my concern would have proven groundless and would leave no more trace of itself, at the end of the day, than a sigh or a shake of the head. Glancing at my watch, I saw that the minute hand was approaching one o'clock. It was the only thing moving in this landscape, as still as it was silent. Something had happened. I just didn't know what it was.

But it was pointless to stand there any longer. Sweat was dampening my hair and my shirt and I felt a headache coming on from so much squinting in the sun. Besides, I thought, I could use some company. I walked the short way back to Philippe and Claire's place, through the gate, across the courtyard, where the dazzling white gravel crunched loudly underfoot, and to the farmhouse, a big stone structure with walls eighteen inches thick and cool even in the middle of summer.

Since lunch had been planned for noon, I expected to find Claire and Philippe waiting, like me, for Susan to show up. They'd probably be in the first room, the main one, which extended the whole length of the house, with a kitchen on the right and a table on the left where people ate or just hung out and where Philippe and I had been working. Right inside the door through which Susan had left on her walk, it was so dark my eyes took ten or fifteen seconds to adjust. But there was no one there. I cocked an ear. Not a sound. I checked the bedroom where we were staying, off to the left, just in case. Then I came back and walked to the stairway at the far end of the room, listening for noises from the second floor—people talking, a chair scraping, running water, footsteps, a bedspring. Nothing. I really didn't have a clue where Philippe could have disappeared to. Come to think of it, I didn't remember Claire returning from her outing, either. In fact I wasn't even sure the two of them were on the property. I was all at sea.

As if reading my mind, Claire suddenly materialized from a side room, holding Augustin by the hand. Augustin was the five-year-old son of Jean-Luc and Hélène, here for a visit while his parents met with doctors back in Strasbourg. He was a handsome dark-haired boy who wanted to be a paleontologist. And he'd been practicing his pronunciation: *pa-lé-on-to-logue*. Five years old, with a big five-syllable dream. But still a boy. What he liked most about the farm was *la mare aux grenouilles*, the frog pond. "The frog pond?" I asked. "I didn't know there was a frog pond!" "Oh yes," replied Claire, adding, as she looked down at Augustin, "since we're waiting to have lunch, why don't you show it to Tom?"

I followed Augustin outside. We turned right, went around the corner of the house, and headed toward the backyard and the field beyond it. How, I wondered, am I going to get into the spirit of this activity? A voice in my head insisted that I pay full attention to Augustin. I had to show enthusiasm for the frog pond, if only to be polite. Another voice, the advocate of magical thinking, countered that I should focus exclusively on Susan to make sure she'd be okay. A third retorted, No, no, it's just the opposite: you have to *not* think about her to ensure her survival. A fourth exclaimed, Survival! Who's talking about survival? Your wife is late for lunch and you think it's the end of the world! You're going to feel like a fool for all your catastrophizing.

While trying to impose some order on this cacophony, I felt a tug on my arm. Augustin pulled me closer and whispered, "The frogs are taking a nap in that long grass by the water. The trick is to sneak up on them. You don't want to scare them off before you get a chance to see what they can do."

We moved with the greatest possible stealth, on tiptoe, trying not to let our shadows fall in the wrong place and give us away. I was just beginning to think those frogs had already taken the plunge when one of them suddenly launched into the air, its parabolic flight ending with a tidy *ploop* out in the water. Augustin and I looked at each other, grinning. Out of curiosity, I did some math.

I assumed the frog measured about ten centimeters from head to tail and had leapt roughly three meters. That was thirty times its own length! Then I visualized, instead of the frog, an Olympic swimmer, assumed a height of 1.8 meters (six feet), and multiplied that by thirty. In this scenario, the starting dive alone would extend fifty-four meters, which meant the swimmer wouldn't even touch the water until the second lap, having executed the first flip turn while still airborne. You had to hand it to the frogs.

We circled the pond, sending a good fifteen of them on their way like this. With running commentary: "Frog Number Six, Monsieur Anatole, has stumbled on takeoff and will not make the finals. But Frog Number Seven, Mademoiselle Angélique, has set a new world record with a leap of 3.2 meters!" We improvised and embellished, each time stretching and kneading and rolling the word for frog, *grenouille*, a word that asks so much of an American mouth I couldn't help giggling along with Augustin. Eventually we took leave of Anatole, Angélique, and friends, including that day's champion, Big Mac. As we retraced our steps toward the house, I thanked Augustin for showing me the frog pond. "Elle est fantastique, ta mare!" I added. With a skip he cried, "Oui, c'est super!"

I don't recall looking at my watch. Maybe I didn't want to know. Or maybe clock time had become irrelevant. I registered the rhythmic *whish-whish* of pant legs against tall grass. I wondered, What next? By chance, Augustin found a stray soccer ball, a bit worse for wear but still serviceable. We'd almost reached the backyard, a good place to kick it around.

I had just sent the ball back to Augustin when from the corner of my eye I caught a sudden movement by the side of the farmhouse. In my countless replayings of this scene, I pause here, lingering on the first sign, the peripheral, split-second sign of what was to come. When I press *play*, I see a man running toward us from the courtyard, calling my name, shouting my name, and I recognize Philippe. It was so strange to see Philippe running. I'd once asked him if he ever exercised and been met with a look suggesting I'd insulted not only his mother but generations of her forebears. His was a life of the mind. If he was running, something was wrong.

Another strange thing: Philippe seemed to be running in place. He was suspended in the air, his legs pumping to no avail, as if some force opposed his forward motion, as if, perhaps, I myself was pushing him back through a sheer effort of will, for fear of what he would say.

He yelled, "Tom, something happened to Susan!"

An ambulance was standing at the gate to the farm, its lights flashing. I tore across the courtyard and leaped from the brilliant sunshine into the darkness of the van. At first I saw nothing but a human form on a stretcher and the outline of an oxygen mask. Next to the stretcher was a medic. He was waiting for me to come closer.

Susan had short blond hair, a smooth, fair complexion, blue-green eyes that sparkled, the gently rounded cheeks of a cherub, an exceptionally winsome smile. And *Susan* was the name I'd just heard. But I didn't recognize the person on the stretcher. What threw me off was the monstrous bulge on her forehead. The cheeks so angrily swollen they left mere slits for her eyes. The skin all discolored by bruises and scratches. The bloodied lips, the hair caked with mud.

She must have seen the terror in my eyes. With a bandaged hand, she slowly lifted the oxygen mask and said, hoarsely, "I'll be okay," which has struck me ever since as an astonishing expression of love. To me, though, it wasn't at all clear she'd be okay. I thought she was going to die. Or suffer permanent brain damage. My first impulse what to ask what happened, yet the question felt so inadequate it just died in my throat. Before replacing the oxygen mask, she asked me to get her glasses. Glasses? In my panic I was momentarily puzzled, even though I knew very well that she always wore glasses or contact lenses. But this was not a time for explanations.

I turned and jumped back out of the ambulance. No sooner had my feet hit the ground than a sudden realization made me raise my arms, clench my fists, flex every muscle I had and some I didn't, lift my chin to the sky—and scream. I knew what this was! I couldn't have said how I knew but I knew. A man had done this. And if it was the last thing I ever did I'd kill him.

As I ran into the house it occurred to me that just then there had been some shapes behind the ambulance, human figures, people I barely perceived. People looking on and, as it happened, watching me scream. Philippe, certainly, and possibly Claire. I just hoped it wasn't Augustin.

But there was no time to dwell on this, no time even to feel ashamed. I raced back into the guest room and searched frantically for the glasses. I was cursing aloud, aware of every second ticking by, then trying, when I found them on a nightstand, not to crush the frames in my fist. I flew out the door, ran across the blazing courtyard, and climbed back into the van. The medic hadn't moved. Susan was still breathing. Somebody bolted the doors behind us.

2 *Emergency*

On the highway, all was quiet except for the low drone of the motor and the hum of the tires against the pavement. Susan was still taking oxygen. The medic was seated to her right, facing her. He kept a close watch but didn't speak unless it was to ask, in a barely audible voice, if she could breathe all right or if she needed to shift her position on the stretcher. I sat to her left, sometimes placing my hand on hers but saying nothing.

Panic set my heart pounding whenever I looked at her. I'd never seen anything like it. I couldn't fathom the hatred capable of visiting this grotesque disfigurement on her lovely face. I also had trouble imagining how anyone who looked as bad as she did could survive.

But the medic was calm. A matter of training, no doubt. How would it have been, after all, if he'd shown even a hint of the tumultuous alarm that threatened to leave my own composure in shambles? Yet his outward poise was so far removed from my inner panic that I found it confusing. I just couldn't connect it to the urgency of Susan's condition. And then maybe his calmness compounded an impression I was already getting from the driver. For although I was pretty sure the ambulance lights were still flashing, I didn't hear a siren, which you would have expected in such an emergency. What's more, I noticed a number of cars passing us. Not that I was at all surprised to see French motorists speeding on the autoroute. But still—shouldn't *we* have been passing *them*?

I tried reasoning with myself: since the man attending to Susan knew so much more about medical emergencies than I did, his calmness might mean that her condition was closer, say, to serious than to critical—that her life wasn't imminently threatened, that things weren't as bad as they looked. This seemed to make sense. Except that just then sense wasn't so obviously in the making. If I couldn't infer from the beauty of the countryside that Susan would be safe going for a walk in it, then I wasn't inclined to assume from the equanimity of an EMT that she was out of danger. Besides, he probably didn't know. He was just doing his job, following the book on first response, and couldn't have offered me the reassurance I craved even if I'd dared to break the silence and ask for it.

Occasionally I glanced outside. From the world passing by you would have sworn we were moving. But it was like being in a train you think is pulling out of the station only to discover you were fooled by the motion of another one pulling in. It was the external world itself that was moving, while the world inside the van was at a standstill.

Having nothing else to do, I circled back to my uncertainty about Susan's condition. Eventually I persuaded myself I'd just have to live with it until we reached the hospital. But in acknowledging this I was bargaining with fate, conceding the delay in exchange for a guarantee that the uncertainty would end just beyond the emergency room doors. Magical thinking again, of a sort. Yet it was the best deal I could get, and made it a little less difficult, right then and there, to sit still and be quiet in the midst of unprecedented calamity. It also helped distract me from another, less immediate but more worrisome challenge, something like a foreboding of despair, the dawning awareness that, even if Susan survived, life would never be the same, and that nothing I could do would mitigate, much less dispel, the awfulness of what had happened.

To my knowledge, though, none of this subjective drama of mine was apparent. The medic, having earlier witnessed me scream, may well have wondered where I'd acquired such self-control. Of course, I didn't need to be told that a husband in hysterics could only worsen a situation that was already bad enough. But I think this surface composure was mostly due to an adaptation going on inside me since I'd climbed back into the ambulance. At that very moment, I detected the triggering of an internal adjustment, not just a change in gears but a change in the way gears are used, as in downshifting, where the motor itself becomes a brake. Maybe whatever remained of the massive dose of adrenaline that produced my scream was suddenly enlisted in the containment of its own impact. For I wasn't being spared the turmoil; it was just that the pressure it exerted seemed to have been turned back against it, so that it didn't show. I was inclined to believe this was all happening at some primitive organic level where my conscious self was just lucky to be granted observer status. Yet I remember very clearly the moment it started, and the sense that an effort of will was involved. As though hearing someone say, "You'd better cool it, or else," I positioned myself in the van and prepared to be, like an actor taking the stage, "in character": the strong, supportive spouse. A man.

Things happened fast when we finally arrived at the hospital in Grenoble—so fast as to banish any doubts about the gravity of the situation. No sooner did the ambulance doors open than we found ourselves rushing down a corridor, Susan lying on the gurney while I strode next to her, holding her hand. We entered a spacious, brightly lit room where she was quickly settled in. The upper half of her bed was raised so she could be better observed. The nurse offered me a stool, which I placed to Susan's left, hoisting myself up to face her.

This combination of emergency room and intensive care unit was where we spent the next thirty hours. Susan was under continuous neurological observation. She wasn't allowed to sleep, even to doze off. She couldn't eat or drink, either, in case they had to administer general anesthesia for an operation. The nurse showed me something I could do to help: I could fill a glass with water, dip the edge of a hand towel in it, and gently dab Susan's chapped and bloodied lips. For this, I needed to lean in close. The first time, there was something about the simple act of leaning that moved me to kiss her on the cheek. Then I caught myself. It would have been a painful kiss. I also detected an odor, the odor of male sweat.

There were blood tests and X rays. A gynecological exam. Visits by an ophthalmologist and an ENT to check her throat. They took twigs from her hair, mud from under her fingernails. At one point a doctor approached to say the enormous swelling on Susan's forehead had to be lanced and drained. He added, apologetically, that neurological concerns prevented him from using even a local anesthetic. When he was done, he wrapped her head in a wide white bandage, making her look like a wounded soldier.

Yet there were lulls, moments when the flurry would suddenly cease and give way to an interval in which nothing happened, in which we just waited. The whole day had been like that. Waiting interminably for her to return from her walk, then sprinting to the ambulance. Waiting for that snail of an ambulance to reach the hospital, then rushing to her room. And now this, as if time could only race or stall. But with no predictable rhythm, no script to follow.

And the trouble with lulls was they gave my mind too much room to roam. We couldn't fill them with conversation, since the damage to Susan's throat made it hard for her to talk. As a result, my imagination ran amok, all the more as her wounds weren't just serious but so numerous that it seemed the attack must have been drawn out. My brain produced, unbidden, snapshot after snapshot, clip after clip of her all alone, fighting for her life and probably expecting to lose it. At moments the relief of being back together could barely hold its own against the distress aroused by these images of absolute abandonment. The only way to dispel them would be to find out what actually took place, to listen to her tell the story. But nobody could say when that would happen.

One thing was certain, if only one: we would not be separated. We were far from the scene of the crime but not from the specter of Susan's assailant, who was still on the loose. She was terrified of being left alone and her fear was contagious. We didn't care if our determination to stay together meant we'd be flouting rules and regulations, norms and protocols. The scare we'd had was so acute as to invest us with absolute authority in the matter. When the gynecologist came to examine Susan, I remained in the room—minding my own business, but in the room. No walls or doors, no circumstances, no person or pretext, not even an executive order from the President of the French Republic—nothing would be allowed to come between us.

During one of these lulls, Susan let me know she wanted her parents to be informed. But the only available telephone was a corded one in the nurses' station next door. From her bed Susan might have been able to hear me, but she couldn't have seen me. A nurse suggested that with one hand I could stretch the cord far enough to wave the other through the doorway. I might have found this bit of vaudeville amusing if I hadn't left my sense of humor at the frog pond. "Okay," said the nurse, "I'll stay with her. I promise."

I might then have fretted about the quality of the connection between Grenoble and Denver if I hadn't been in a quandary over something else. What was I going to say? I'd never been the bearer of such bad news. I'd never been a parent. I had no guidelines. And how much did I really know? I knew Susan had been sexually assaulted. The gynecological exam and the smell I picked up only confirmed what had hit me as I leaped out of the ambulance. When I asked her, years later, whether she recalled a moment at which she'd told me in so many words, she replied, "You didn't need to be told. Telling would only have been necessary if *you* had been the one on the stretcher." But this was also the one thing she didn't want me to tell her parents. Not yet, anyway.

So, should I just describe the wounds I could see? They were so many and so severe it would have seemed pointless, even cruel. Yet how much information could I withhold without feeling dishonest? How many euphemisms, how much circumlocution could I resort to before it became condescending? What if I downplayed the story so much that they and everybody they relayed it too were seriously misled? And how would I bring this dreaded call to a close?

Entering the nurses' station felt like trespassing. Among so many immaculate white uniforms, my grimy, wrinkled tee shirt made it embarrassingly clear I didn't belong. As I looked around, though, trying to locate the telephone, it struck me that everything in the nurses' station—not only the uniforms but the brisk, purposeful movements and steady voices, the neatly arranged medical supplies, the charts and files—everything spoke of an order about as foreign and fascinating as could be for someone living, like me, in chaos. There, too, at the center of the unit, I could see that ours was just one scene in today's drama, that Susan was just one of the patients they were attending to during this shift and might well be replaced by another when they reported to work tomorrow. For us, what had happened bore no comparison to anything else. For them, Susan was a case to be handled according to a general know-how acquired in medical or nursing school. Then, when I picked up the receiver—resisting the temptation, in my benumbed state, to simply gaze at it, as if I'd just smoked a joint—I paused to calculate the hour in Denver. Not once had I thought about clock time since hearing Philippe's cry. Not once had I stopped to consider that other people were just going about their daily routine. People in Denver, checking their dashboard dials as they crawled through traffic toward another day at work. Yet people right there in Grenoble as well. People everywhere. The whole world was revolving atop the tacit and incredibly tenuous assumption that life was shared and ongoing. I'd simply never seen this from the outside, where no such assumption was possible, and where all the clocks had stopped.

Bob and Martha would be sitting in the breakfast area between the kitchen and the TV room, with a view of the lake just beyond the backyard of their suburban house. They'd be savoring their oatmeal, checking headlines from the *Denver Post*, exchanging a few words about the day ahead. If the weather was favorable, Bob might do some windsurfing on the lake. Martha would have a painting class or be planning to visit neighbors in their close-knit community. These kind, gentle people would just be sitting there, minding their own business, when the phone rang. One of them would answer in the kitchen, and, hearing it was me, would have the other pick up in the bedroom. Before I said a word about the attack, I would already have sent a message. For I disliked the telephone. At home, I seldom if ever initiated a call to them. Why would I call from France? At the mere sound of my voice, their pulse was bound to quicken. This was going to hurt.

I've forgotten all the details of this conversation except one. I do recall the general sense of walking an informational tightrope, maintaining my balance through a kind of echolocation, leaning correctively this way or that depending on the response to what I'd just said. If I heard too much optimism, I'd gently emphasize that Susan's head wounds were serious. If I heard too much alarm, I'd make another adjustment, promising to keep them posted and thus hoping to dispel any doubts about her survival.

But all of this was eclipsed by a very brief exchange toward the end, triggered when Bob wondered aloud if he could ask a question. "Sure," I replied, reluctantly, perhaps suspecting what was coming. "Go ahead."

"Well, uh . . . was she raped?"

"No."

"Oh, oh, I see. So there was no rape?"

"No."

I lied calmly, disguising as best I could a sudden indignation. My wife had almost been killed and could still die. If she survived, there was a risk of brain damage. She was so shaken she couldn't bear to have me leave her side, and I was making an exception in order to place this call. What did it matter, right then, whether she'd been raped or not when her very life was at stake? And so what if I hadn't conveyed the full gravity of her condition! I'd been trying to protect them. More than that, I'd been protecting Susan. Having lost all control of her life, she felt the need at least to control her story, to decide who knew, how much, and when. Even if Bob thought it likely she'd been raped, was it too much to ask that he trust her (or me) to speak of it when she was ready?

Susan may also have suspected that her parents, as a matter of character and background, were not especially well-equipped to understand what she'd suffered and to support her in its aftermath. As it turned out, this suspicion was not unfounded. Which is not to say that Bob and Martha were uncaring: we later learned that, after saying goodbye to me, they'd hugged each other and sobbed. But being a caring person doesn't necessarily mean being attuned to the experience of a trauma victim. The call left me not only depleted but with the impression that this relationship so central to our lives was already strained.

At more settled moments, though, I considered whether it was entirely fair to blame Bob for broaching the subject of rape. If Susan had been my daughter, wouldn't I have asked the same question? Or at least wanted to? For that matter, when I jumped out of the ambulance, what was it I'd realized with such strange certainty if not what occurred to my father-in-law once I'd alluded to the beating? And as Susan walked out the door that morning, why, really, was I so worried? Had I been the one taking a walk, she would've had no cause for concern. What Bob's question had done was expose a tacit assumption we shared about men and that made me feel, under the circumstances, more implicated than ever in a world where that assumption was justified on a daily basis.

Maybe it was to counteract this feeling of complicity in a crime I hadn't committed that I wanted to track Susan's assailant down and administer the thrashing he so richly deserved. Kill him, in other words. Being in no position to do so doubtless wedded me more firmly to the fantasy, where I could unleash my rage in complete disregard of any practical consequences. I didn't even have to ask myself how such revenge could possibly change the culture that had facilitated his crime in the first place. Or whether the recourse to violence wouldn't further entangle me in the very masculinity I loathed. But I must also have known that this imaginary retaliation would have no effect on my real sense of complicity. The rage itself was an admission of powerlessness—the powerlessness to prevent what was inflicted on Susan by someone of my own gender.

That evening, I noticed the arrival of a new team of doctors and nurses. The night shift. I glanced at my watch. Sure enough, it was late. For most people, the day would soon be over. Tomorrow would be another day. They'd go to sleep with some sense of an ending and wake up with some sense of a beginning. July 4 would give way to July 5, and the world would move on.

For us, it would be a white night. Susan would be kept awake. So would I. This wasn't up to us, but it didn't matter since we were already carrying a potent strain of insomnia. Not the common variety, which is unpleasant enough but arises from anxiety about something *in* life: problems at work, family conflicts, health issues, money. Our insomnia was about life as such—whether it would even continue or not. What happened that morning disrupted the whole rhythm of our existence, stranding us in the anarchic interval following an explosion, an earsplitting blast that blew the familiar *tick tock* all to hell. We were stunned, and bound to stay that way for a while. It would have been great to close our eyes, drift away, forget, just for a minute or two. Even to have a nightmare we could wake up from.

Can I get away with saying "we" as I just did? I'd never been through anything like what Susan had suffered, which meant that, even in the hospital, her experience and mine were not the same. Who am I to speak for her? It may be that, when I recall those first thirty hours, "we" comes readily to my lips as a response to our having almost been severed from each other, permanently. Like an emergency measure. A suture.

Still, that she was alive didn't rule out the possibility that something had really been lost. I'd had an inkling of this in the ambulance, a sense that everything as we knew it, including who we were, was gone for good. The malaise returned at one point in the hospital, when I happened to pull a piece of paper from my back pocket. Creased, wrinkled, smudged. On it was the itinerary I'd typed up before leaving home, with all the dates, locations, people, and phone numbers for our trip, which had just begun when the assault took place. Now, it looked like a relic. Like a scrap I could imagine someday coming across while sorting through a box in the attic, reminding me of hopes and plans foiled long ago, and clipped to an old close-up photograph of us looking straight at the camera, our gaze mesmerizing because so unsuspecting.

But "we" also pointed to the future, as foreshortened as it may have seemed. It was like a bet that we made against formidable odds (since, as we later learned from clinicians, most couples in a situation like ours didn't manage to stay together). Or like a placeholder, reserved for as long as we needed it to answer the question, "Who's 'we'"?

Around mid-morning on July 5, I got my first look at Susan's assailant. We'd gone twenty-four hours without sleep or anything to eat or drink and were in a daze when suddenly a man walked into the room unannounced. He was clearly not a member of the medical staff. And by then I'd come to share Susan's belief that her attacker could be roaming the hospital corridors. Only a state of utter depletion prevented me from jumping off my stool and swinging it at him. It also spared me arrest for assaulting a police officer.

This plainclothes detective carried a large briefcase and a thick ring binder. Pulling up a chair to Susan's right, he asked her to look through the binder and tell him if she recognized her assailant in any of the photographs. She sat up, adjusted her glasses, and focused on the album. This was not the first time she'd surprised me. The first was when, in the ambulance, she'd had the presence of mind to ask for the glasses she was now wearing. (Only later, during her deposition, did I realize how losing her contact lenses during the attack had compounded her terror.) Now, watching her attend to the task at hand, I had to believe she'd found a source of strength or resolve I didn't know about, and maybe even she didn't know about, never having had to draw on it before.

As she turned the pages, I was amazed by the sheer number of candidates. Dozens and dozens of them. And these were just the ones who got caught. Or convicted. If only I'd known of this crowd, I'd have found a way to dissuade her from taking that walk. If only, to begin with, Claire had taken her on that promised outing. Or if only, setting out on her walk, Susan had turned left instead of right. If only we'd never come here. If only.

She leafed her way carefully through the binder. Whenever a face arrested her attention, I found myself glued to the image, wondering. I kept thinking she'd extend her index finger, point to a photo, and say, "That's him." But no. Perhaps he was a first offender.

The detective set the binder aside and lifted his briefcase. Inside was something I'd never seen before: an Identi-Kit, used to produce a facial composite, or *portrait-robot*. For each feature—hair and forehead; ears, eyes, and nose; mouth and chin—there was a large series of sketches. You'd choose one from each series, move to the next series, and so on until you'd assembled the whole face. Susan couldn't have worked on it more studiously. It must have taken well over an hour. The detective was very patient and didn't let on that he knew anything. In the meantime, I was totally engrossed, watching the attacker's face materialize, little by little, as if in an extended-release Polaroid.

The hair was dark, almost shoulder-length, unkempt. So much for my preconception. For some reason I'd expected a resemblance to the drunk from Talloires. My brain must have done a search of *French Criminals I've Known* and come up with the only item in the file. That guy was blond. And he had blue eyes, whereas the eyes of the developing *portrait-robot* were dark, like the hair. Once Susan had selected the mouth and the chin, the face as a whole appeared round and fleshy, suggesting attachment to a stocky physique, the kind you might associate with an NFL lineman.

As the detective packed up his equipment, a second man entered the room. I stayed on my stool, trusting in the police protection we already had. The two of them stood off to one side, and I noticed the new guy take one look at the facial composite and nod his head. Before leaving, they let it be known that Susan was a superb portraitist. They may have added, or I may just have inferred, that her work would allow them to make an arrest.

I remember, toward the end of our stay in the ER/ICU, the gritty eyes. I remember the cognitive impairment and the stiffness in my joints, which made me feel, atop my stool, like a dunce with arthritis. I remember the headache that came and went, leaving me unsure if I really had it or if it was just playing Tweedledum to the Tweedledee of a dizziness that threatened every now and then to tip me right off my perch. What I don't remember is when we learned that Susan would survive. Was there ever such a moment? If so, how did we react? We couldn't have jumped for joy. What would we have jumped for joy *with*? You don't spend so many hours in the grim proximity of death, deprived of all sleep and caloric intake, only to find yourself dancing to life's promise.

The message must have gotten across less through what the medical personnel said than through what they did. What they did was to start planning for Susan to be transferred to another unit. Admittedly, this wasn't the same as a clean bill of health. But it strongly suggested that she was out of danger.

And we were lucky. Susan's brother, a radiology technician in Denver, had a connection at the hospital. A Dr. Jean-Paul Stahl, who might be able to help us with the room. When our nurse called his office, he not only answered the phone himself but invited me to drop by right away. I couldn't even imagine this happening in the United States.

There was a hitch, though. Dr. Stahl's office was on another floor. Again, as when I'd had to leave Susan's bedside to call her parents, we persuaded a nurse to stay with her. My walking out the door nonetheless required a huge leap of faith for both of us.

Heading down the hallway toward the elevator, I was on the lookout for Susan's attacker. I sensed no fear on my own account, only a steely determination to do him in if he showed up. And what a gruesome scene that would be! All heedless ferocity on my part, gnashing teeth and snarled curses, blood and gore. I was still engrossed in this when I passed a nurse who gave me a quizzical, slightly worried glance, as if such thoughts had contorted my posture or my facial expression, making me look like a stray from the psychiatric ward. Pausing just long enough to realize I'd walked right by the elevator, I turned on my heels, retraced my steps, and flashed the same nurse a smile that may simply have confirmed her first impression by suggesting sudden and severe mood swings. But once there, I found my mind veering off in a completely different direction, related to the occupation of confined spaces with other people. For my clothes were rumpled, my hair was dirty, I hadn't shaved, and I was feeling far from fragrant. Even if I offended no one in the elevator, what if Dr. Stahl's office wasn't big enough for him to keep me at arm's length?

He listened patiently as I told him the story. Then I made my pitch: Would it be possible for Susan to have a private room? He just nodded, smiling. I was taken aback, and could barely manage to stammer my thanks. I was already having enough trouble figuring out the forces of evil. Were the forces of good equally opaque? But Dr. Stahl just maintained his air of imperturbable benevolence. Making my way back to the elevator, I tried to recall when or where I'd heard somebody talking about charity. Somebody who said that, far from being sentimental, true charity is efficient.

In the course of those thirty hours, Susan's face changed. Around the time the hematoma on her forehead was lanced, it appeared that the swelling in her cheeks was going down, too. She was becoming recognizable again, much to my relief. But then the bruises on her face and neck, an array of muted yellows, greens, and purples, grew more vivid, until they'd attained a positively Day-Glo fluorescence, making it look like she'd just played a game of paintball. In the meantime, this splash of color distracted attention from a slower-paced development that would eventually outdo the bruises: by late afternoon on July 5, the whites of her eyes had turned, in their entirety, a bright crimson.

I queried the medical personnel about the bruises. They told me that this neon rainbow was part of the healing process—in essence, that the bruises looked worse because Susan was getting better. Later, when a nurse detected my alarm at the spectacle of Susan's eyes, she made a well-intentioned effort to comfort me, commenting, "Oh, that's just an effect of strangulation."

By eight p.m. we were in our own room. Oddly enough, in the section for contagious diseases. But who cared? This was where Dr. Stahl managed to find us a room. It was at the end of a corridor on an upper story of the building, with a window that looked out on the hospital parking lot. There was a small table with two chairs, a bathroom, and a cot for me next to Susan's bed.

The door to the room didn't lock from the inside. And in any case the staff, who had greeted us very warmly, wanted it left open so they could keep an eye on Susan. They must have been briefed by the people downstairs, since they took the trouble to assure us that there was no way in the world Susan's assailant would come looking for her at the hospital. We smiled politely. Until bedtime, I stood sentinel by the door, watching the hallway, which was very long and mostly deserted.

Around then a young nurse came in, exuding a liveliness we'd find all the more endearing when later in our stay, working the day shift, she'd confide to us that she'd been out dancing till dawn. She offered us a sedative called Lexomil—and with it, the first rest we'd have since Susan was almost killed. We were grateful. To her, and even more to the drug. So much so that I was inspired to compose a poem entitled "Ode to Lexomil." But the potion acted too fast, and I drifted away, telling myself that the literary world would be better off without it.

3 *Interlude*

The next morning, we asked about taking a bath. As I took the handles of Susan's wheelchair, a nurse guided us down the hallway to a door on the left, then ushered us into a tiled room in the center of which stood a tub that was outsized even by European standards. Behind it was an enclosure with a showerhead. Towels and soap were provided. Shampoo as well. I would hardly have been surprised if the nurse had offered us emblazoned terrycloth robes and a selection of New Age soundscapes.

Like the other medical personnel, she must have been briefed about our fears, since she made a point of saying we could lock the door from the inside. Which is what I did as soon as she left. Then, striding to the bathtub, I flicked my wrist as decisively as an orchestra conductor—and released a startling blast of good hot water. Grinning, I recalled those old black-and-white photographs of uncapped hydrants in the hot summer streets of New York. At last I could *do* something for Susan, even though she could have done it for herself. But I insisted: "Permettez-moi, Madame!" While I checked out the room, she rose from her wheelchair and slipped slowly into the water, taking pleasure in the buoyancy, the effortless floating. The lift.

With a small brush for cleaning under nails, Susan worked on her fingers, including two fractured ones that had been temporarily unsplinted. Then she handed me the brush and I prepared to work on her toes. I was kneeling at the far end of the tub, looking up at her face. Gone was the broad bandage circling her head and making her look like a combat casualty (which, in a sense, she was). Her cheeks had almost returned to their enchanting contours. And now, fortified by an optimistic prognosis, I found the reds of her eyes and her motley crew of bruises to be less alarming than, well, colorful.

All the same, I felt I should have something more to offer her than a good scrub. Something more inventive. It came to me suddenly, probably in connection with the "Permettez-moi, Madame!" Courtly love! A poetic address, drawing on the little I'd retained from a long-ago graduate course. What about the music, though? The first thing that sprang to mind was one of the sappiest popular tunes ever recorded, "You Needed Me." Yet I had to find new lyrics to get away from the original schmaltz. The piece I created, called "You Think I Stink," was about a forlorn guy who roamed the aisles of countless pharmacies in search of a deodorant to spare his Lady's sensibility, and the failure of whose quest turned him from a knight-errant into a troubadour. The whole thing came together with scarcely a moment's reflection. The meter was spot-on, the rhyme perfect, the narrative development flawless. It was a chef d'oeuvre that made Susan laugh for the first time.

While she soaked, I walked over to the shower. I could hardly get my soiled clothes off fast enough. I turned on the water, adjusted the temperature, and pulled the curtain almost flush to the wall. Almost, because I was still on guard. The door to the room was locked from our side, and even a shout of moderate volume would have brought the staff to our assistance. It didn't matter. We still had one foot squarely planted in a universe where anything could happen. Every fifteen or twenty seconds, I poked my head out and scanned the room.

In the brief intervals, I took pleasure in flushing the grime from my skin. I tilted my head back, letting the warm water splash all over my face as I imagined it washing away the years I'd aged in just the past two days. But while rinsing off, I happened to look down, and froze. For a split second, what I saw was a body completely detached and depersonalized. A body that could have belonged to any man. A living, if headless, anatomical model. Yet also an indictment, the proof of *my* complicity, in the flesh and therefore inescapable. A body not of my choice but mine nonetheless, with the standard genitals and a natural inclination to produce smells of the kind left by the rapist, which no shower could eradicate from my memory.

I didn't tell Susan. I didn't know, myself, what to make of such a strange epiphany. But from then on, I wondered how I could ever let her love this body of mine again even if she wanted to.

4 *The Assault*

We spent ten more days in the hospital. At first it was a challenge for Susan just to get her legs over the side of the bed, then stand, then swivel into her wheelchair or, at most, walk with assistance. In addition to her other injuries, she had a fractured trachea and a detached vitreous. Her nerves had been strained to the limit. All of this was preoccupying enough that I seldom stopped to consider how certain caregiving measures took me into account.

Every night I was allowed to sleep on a cot beside her bed, for instance. I wasn't exiled to some corner, dozing fitfully on a recliner. I had my own cot, where I could actually sleep and from which, at any moment, I could reach up and touch Susan's hand over the rail of the hospital bed. The cot stayed in the room the whole time, folded up during the day. What's more, all meals were served for two, and Lexomil was dispensed to the spouse as well as to the patient. In other circumstances, this arrangement would have seemed irregular. If Susan had just undergone an appendectomy, I doubt very much that provision would have been made for me to sleep next to her or be served the same food—much less receive the same medication! These things suggested a diagnosis of sorts, or at least an awareness of the social psychology of trauma.

For it was Susan's non-physical wounds that required my physical presence. And why else would I, with no physical injury, have been treated so much like a patient?

But I didn't really take it in at the time. If I'd given any thought to these measures, I would have chalked them up to institutional pragmatism, enhanced by the generosity of the French healthcare system. It didn't occur to me to see them as an informed response to secondary trauma, or to make any connection between the symptoms they treated and my moment of dissociation in the shower. Because this wasn't about me. The assistance I received simply made it easier to be the supportive spouse.

Later on the day of the bath, the second detective came by. He was the man who'd shown up right after Susan finished the facial composite. Unlike the first detective, who'd sat with her while she worked on it, he'd already seen the suspect and could judge the conformity of the composite to the real face. Just before we left the ER/ICU, he'd returned by himself, holding up a photograph and asking Susan if she recognized her assailant in it. She did.

We hadn't expected to see him a third time. Now he brought a series of photographs that suggested the equivalent of a police lineup. It included the photograph Susan had already seen. When he asked her to select her assailant from the series, she complied, trying not to convey her impression that there was something peculiar about the procedure. Wasn't this identification a bit odd, resembling as it did a multiple-choice question to which she'd already given the answer? Was it just a test to make doubly sure she got the right guy? Although the confusion I shared with her may have clouded our perception, it seemed to both of us that the detective himself was slightly flustered.

What we knew about criminal justice amounted to no more than what most people knew and was derived from the same informal sources: television, movies, newspapers, magazines, hearsay. In other words, not much. And even that was restricted to the U.S. Now we were in a foreign country, which we knew fairly well in some respects but where our passing acquaintance with the American judicial system would be of still less avail than at home. We wondered whether the detective had made a mistake. Could there be a mistrial based on such a technicality?

Susan's first deposition was scheduled for July 7. On the evening of the 6th, she surprised me yet again. Less than three days had passed since the attack—and now she sat propped up in her bed, her glasses on, the picture of studiousness with a pen in her hand and a pad of paper on her lap, writing notes to herself for more than an hour. "You know," she said at one point, looking up, "this reminds me of preparing for my PhD dissertation defense."

Claire would be there for the deposition. A native speaker of French with a good command of English, she could help resolve any linguistic difficulties that arose. She'd be driving into Grenoble in her old green Mercedes station wagon. It was thanks to this car that they found me before taking Susan to the hospital. None of her rescuers knew who Claire and Philippe were or where they lived, so Susan's insistence on seeing me before all else was at first in vain. But then she mentioned the car, which, it turned out, the medic had occasionally seen parked at the house. Neither of us had ever ridden in it, but it ended up bringing us back together. I didn't even want to think about what the day would have been like without it—for Susan, surrounded by strangers and transported to Grenoble with no way of reaching me; for me, more convinced with every passing minute that I'd never see her alive again.

Early on the morning of the 7th, after Claire had arrived, the three of us heard a discreet knock at the door. A gendarme in uniform entered the room and introduced himself. He was remarkably young and kind of bashful, but solidly built, as you might expect of a gendarme. He toted a mechanical typewriter and a folding table just large enough to accommodate it, along with a folding chair on which he'd be sitting for the next eight hours.

He rolled a first sheet of paper into the machine and began to enter basic information: date, time, and place of deposition; victim's name, sex, date of birth, nationality, civil status, profession. All of this with just his index fingers, one at a time. The pace suited me, since I was transcribing Susan's story by hand at my own little table. But what follows is the official typed deposition, which I translated from the French and from which I quote with Susan's permission:

> On July 4th, at about 10:30 in the morning, I decided to go for a walk in the area of St.-Etienne-de-St.-Geoirs, where my husband and I were staying with friends. Leaving the house, I turned right and followed the road there for about forty-five minutes. I crossed through a village and continued walking on the road that was directly ahead of me. Ten minutes or so later, I noticed some wild strawberries by the left side of the road. I crossed over, picked a few, ate them, then crossed back and kept walking. Shortly after, I noticed a man standing at the entrance to a narrow dirt road on the left. I thought maybe the strawberries were on his property and he disapproved of my taking them so while continuing to walk I said

> hello politely. He said hello back, in a low and not very friendly voice. I figured he was working in the fields and just happened to be there.
>
> I walked about ten more yards and was suddenly seized from behind. The person put both arms around my throat and squeezed really hard. I struggled and said, "Let me go!" At that point he put a hand over my mouth. He was slightly to my left, his face close to mine, and I could see it was the man I'd just passed. Holding me tight, he dragged me onto the ground behind some bushes about ten feet to the right of the road.
>
> I was on my back and he sat on me and punched me very hard on the left cheek to keep me from fighting back. The punch knocked out my contact lens. At this point I realized he intended to rape me. When he forced himself on me orally I was suffocating and thought of biting him but I was afraid that would make him even more furious than he already was. Recalling what I knew about rapists I thought that if I resisted I could lose my life. He started giving me orders in a gestapo-like voice and called me a whore.

Now and then Susan would pause to rest her voice. Sometimes she'd check her notes or consult with Claire. While she spoke I was preoccupied with writing down what she said. Although there was a point to this task—making sure we had a record of our own—it may also have spared me taking in too much of an unbearable story I was hearing for the first time. I don't recall what I did during the pauses. But one thing was already clear from Susan's account: this guy had been playing a role. He hadn't come up with the gestapo-like voice or the trite epithet *whore* (*putain*) all by himself. He'd found a ready-made narrative, whether in a porn video or in the culture at large. This is how you acted when you raped somebody. So much for the notion of the rapist as a lone, deviant individual.

> The next thing he did was unbuckle my belt, unzip my fly, and pull down my pants and underwear. He spread my legs but I resisted and he didn't succeed in penetrating me. I lied and told him I had a sexually transmitted disease, thinking he'd be sensible enough not to want to get AIDS. I thought I could reason with him, that while violent he wasn't crazy. He just said he didn't give a damn. So then I told him I had my period, hoping this would discourage him. I dug my nails into his testicles and realized he didn't have an erection. He punched me again in the same place and tried to strangle me. I tried to fight back but I was suffocating and lost consciousness.
>
> When I came to I was really scared because he knew how to strangle a person. I talked to him. I said, "Please don't kill me. I'll do whatever you want, tell me what you want, Monsieur." Whenever I spoke to him I ended by saying Monsieur. He seemed to reflect. He ordered me to climb down into the ravine, which was fifteen or twenty feet deep. To do that I had to pull my jeans back up. I thought to myself that the only reason he wants me to do this is to kill me. When we got down there he ordered me, still with the gestapo voice, to get on my knees. I was wondering if he'd been reading porn books or watching violent movies. When I was on my knees he ordered me to put my head down. He went behind me and I thought maybe he was going to take off because I couldn't see him. But instead he strangled me with both hands until I passed out.

"I dug my nails into his testicles." Just before the trial, two and a half years later, we were called into the judge's chambers. For some reason, the *avocat général* (public prosecutor) decided to show Susan some photos that would be shared with the jurors. She was struck by one shot in particular, which showed the serious lacerations she'd inflicted. Proof of how she'd fought back.

And then: "He knew how to strangle a person." Toward the end of the trial, in his summation, the *avocat général* referred to forensic evidence according to which the damage to Susan's hyoid bone signaled the intent to kill, contradicting the defense's claim that the assailant wasn't in control of his actions. I had to look up *hyoid bone*. Wikipedia didn't exist then but here's what you can read now: "Due to its position, the hyoid bone is not easily susceptible to fracture. In a suspected case of murder of an adult, a fractured hyoid bone strongly indicates strangulation." We later learned that the assailant had completed his military service. Probably that's where he learned how to kill.

> When I came to he was a bit farther up the little stream that flowed at the bottom of the ravine. He was looking for a rock. I saw him pick one up, as big as a melon. He came at me and smashed it into my forehead. I lost consciousness again. When I revived I noticed that I'd lost my right contact lens. He had picked up an enormous rock but I moved my head and it missed me. He picked up another, smaller one and I was even more aware that he was intent not on rape but on murder. I pleaded with him several times, saying, "Don't kill me!" I tried to talk with him. He dropped the rock but ordered me to stay on my knees with my head down and my eyes closed. But I didn't dare close my eyes and kept them open. Then I saw him try to pull a fallen tree trunk out of the ground so he could hit me with it. But he couldn't lift it.

I pleaded with him some more, asking him to let me live. I tried again to reason with him. I said, "I'm American and I'm leaving today and won't tell anyone." He asked me if I'd tell my family. I said, "No, I'm by myself, and if anybody asks I'll them I was in a car accident, so it's better if you get away now so nobody will know." I repeated that I wouldn't tell anyone. Several times I said, "I swear!" He thought for a moment and then told me to shut up.

I was still on all fours in the mud, he was behind me, and he tried to strangle me again. Every time I felt like I was dying. I couldn't feel any more air getting through. You can't imagine anything more terrifying than that. Every time he strangled me I tried to rip his hands away, and this time I managed to get two of my fingers between his hands and my neck so I could get a little more air. That helped me breathe a little longer. I think that's why those fingers are smashed. Then I passed out again.

When I came to he ordered me to keep walking up the ravine. All these things took place almost all the time in the mud of the stream. We were headed upstream and must have walked about twenty-five or thirty feet. I noticed the slope on the left was getting steeper and that it would be harder to climb back up to the road. I figured he was doing this to make it more difficult for me to escape. He was a few yards behind me when he thought he heard something and said "Shush!" and spread his arms as a signal to stop. I noticed this because I never took my eyes off him while we were walking. He said, "I hear something up on the road."

"Shush! I hear something up on the road." So intent was I on my transcription that the absurdity of this moment didn't immediately register. Was he really expecting her to cooperate? Did he think they were in this together? How else to explain his deep sense of betrayal at what she did next?

> He wasn't moving, and there was a little more distance between us. I thought this was my last chance to escape. I started climbing up the slope to the left and I yelled as loudly as I could. I really screamed, three or four times. He came running at me, furious. He grabbed me, I continued pleading with him to let me live. I said, "Don't kill me, please!" He just said, "It's necessary,"[1] repeating it several times with the gruff voice he'd had since the beginning. I told him it would be better to stop because I had friends who would come looking for me. He got even madder, he said, "You're a liar, you said you were alone!"

"You're a liar!" She'd violated not only the spirit of cooperation but the basic bond of trust. Yet wasn't that just like a woman! All women were whores and all whores were liars. That, too, was part of the ready-made narrative.

> He ordered me to get on my knees again, head down, my sweat shirt over my head. I thought he was either going to kill me with a rock or let me go. I also thought he had me put the sweatshirt over my head so I couldn't see where he went when he left. But instead he positioned himself behind me and suffocated me by covering my nose and stuffing the sweatshirt into my mouth. I tried to push him away so I could breathe. I was in such pain, I thought it would be better if I just died. But then I thought of my husband. I didn't want my husband to find me dead in the ravine and be all alone in the world. That gave me the courage to go on.

At this point Susan looked at the gendarme and asked if it was appropriate to mention her husband as she just had. The gendarme replied that it certainly was since the suspect had claimed under interrogation that she'd provoked him into having sex with her in the woods. So there it was again—the narrative cliché.

> He left me lying in the mud. He walked back down in the middle of the stream. I stayed in that position, listening to him move away, not moving so he'd think I was dead. When I thought he was far enough away, I looked in the direction he'd gone. I couldn't see very well but I thought he was far enough away so I could escape by pulling myself up the slope to the left. It was really steep and I had to grab onto bushes and saplings to get up it. I made it to the edge of the road but since I was afraid he might see me I kept down. I hid in some bushes and tall grass, waiting for a car to come by. But none did and I was afraid the man would retrace his steps and find me.
>
> After a while I got up and ran up the road, on the right side, as fast as I could. I could hardly see because my left eye was almost closed and I could see very little with my right eye. The whole time I was afraid I'd pass out. I stopped at the first house I saw on the right, there was a path to the front door but nobody was there. The dogs barked a lot. I came back to the road, I walked a little, then I saw a tractor coming at me. I positioned myself in the middle of the road, my arms out to force him to stop. The tractor took me to the next house, where they called the ambulance.

It was four or five in the afternoon when the gendarme finished plunking on his keyboard, pulled the last sheet of paper out of the machine, and handed the complete typescript to Susan for her to review and sign.

She balked when she saw that a first sentence had been added (omitted above): "I'm athletic, and I like to walk a lot." This was something she'd never said. What was it doing there? Had he slipped it in when we thought he was just entering personal data? Why would he have taken the liberty of putting words in her mouth?

She was tired, however. By then she'd been deposing for eight hours. Should she really insist that it be deleted? On a mechanical typewriter with no Wite-Out available? Would anybody bother to fact-check "I'm athletic, and I like to walk a lot"? She signed.

Still, it was odd. On reflection, it struck us as an attempt at narrative motivation. It seemed designed to appeal to the pervasive French assumption that Americans were crazy about exercise, and so perhaps to forestall the victim-blaming question of what this young woman was up to out walking by herself on a remote country road. But who knew what the gendarme was thinking?

A few days later, after the second deposition Susan gave from her hospital bed, this time before an investigating magistrate, she was asked once again to read the typescript and sign it. At the end of the form was the printed statement: "The photograph of my assailant has been shown to me twice, once by itself and once among others. Both times, I recognized him." As it turned out, then, we'd had no reason to worry about a mistrial based on a technicality, since the detective had been following procedure to the letter. Yet the relief we felt on learning that things were on track was accompanied by the very awareness of our ignorance. What barely qualifies as an anecdote today suggested back then that the French system was constructing a narrative we wouldn't always understand or control, a narrative on which would depend not only the outcome of the case but its repercussions. For although Susan had survived the attack, whether the attacker was held accountable or not was bound to affect her survival of the aftermath.

When I saw Susan on the stretcher I wanted to ask, right away, what happened. I stifled the question, overwhelmed by the sheer magnitude of her suffering and the fear for her life. Now I knew the answer. But since then I've asked myself why I remember so little of what was happening to me as I listened to her.

There were distractions, for sure. I was intensely focused on the accurate recording of her story with a view to its purpose: this was a chance for Susan to reclaim her voice after being so brutally silenced and to play an active role in determining whether justice was done. The stakes were high. In comparison, my feelings were unimportant (or so I thought). And then, just as stenographers aren't called upon to think about what they type, or just as translators are commonly expected to remain invisible, so it was incumbent on me to avoid any interference with the transmission. I needed to stay out of the picture.

All of this was in keeping with the internal adjustment I'd made in the ambulance, which excluded anything that might impair my caregiving capacity. But there was one exception that day—the day of the first deposition—a moment I do recall from listening to Susan, when this adjustment of mine was seriously strained. It was when she brought me into the picture by evoking the image of my face on discovering her body. The gendarme typed: "But then I thought of my husband. I didn't want my husband to find me dead in the ravine and be all alone in the world." Yet Susan hadn't just "thought" of her husband. She'd definitely referred to the image of my face. And if it's possible at one and the same time to be brought to tears and have the breath sucked out of you, that's what happened to me. It wasn't just that I imagined her kneeling in the mud, with this murderer's hands around her throat, trying desperately to stay on this side of death's door. It was also that, earlier, in real time—at the very moment she was fighting for her life, the same moment when I stood out at that junction of dirt roads, wondering where she could be—I'd been unable to restrain my cascading alarm from conjuring the image of her dead body.

As for the rest, I knew it had registered somewhere within me. I couldn't really have said whether my reaction to the story Susan told—a mix of fear, horror, outrage, and sadness—seemed for now to be largely suspended or postponed because of that adjustment of mine or because, like the question I'd stifled, it had been relegated to the sidelines by the enormity of the event itself. But there was no doubt that this unhinging of effect from cause carried a feeling all its own, a sense that none of the emotional, psychological, or cognitive resources I could draw on would ever enable me to catch up to what was supposedly behind us. As far as I could tell, time would always be out of joint.

5 *Still Here*

I felt deep down, like a bass line emerging through rests in the upper registers, a kind of bereavement. True, I had not lost Susan. She was still here. What's more, she'd kept on fighting in order to spare me the worst bereavement of all. Yet surely she'd left more than her favorite belt in that ravine. Something of herself, or some self of hers, was still there and always would be. Defining this "something" would have been as difficult as describing my own sadness, and for the same reason: it was too soon. No doubt this is why the bereavement felt oddly anticipatory. What we'd lost was a discovery that still lay ahead.

In the meantime, we were kept busy. Nurses were constantly coming and going. On his rounds, Dr. Stahl paid a visit, accompanied by some younger colleagues (this was a teaching hospital). With the help of Dr. Catherine Stahl (his spouse), we hired a lawyer. We got a phone for the room.

Every evening I'd sit at our little table and make a list of things to do. More than once I leaned back, in the daze that was fast becoming my default condition, and thought of what I'd heard somebody say about the recently widowed. It was suggested that the host of practical matters requiring attention in the immediate aftermath of a spouse's death worked to the advantage of the survivor by leaving little time to plumb the depths of grief. I wasn't sure I believed that. Although my situation wasn't quite the same, I saw enough of a resemblance to entitle me to an opinion, which was that grief would still submerge you and that the fatigue it occasioned could well convert those practical matters, whether large or small, into tasks that even the strongest of people would find Sisyphean. Or was it Herculean? Overwhelming, in any case.

Take our departure, for example. I mean our eventual departure from the hospital. Not a day went by without my gazing out the window at the parking lot. It was usually sunny out there, making it easy to spot the only turquoise car, a brand new Renault compact. That was our rental car, which Philippe had driven into Grenoble so we'd have it whenever Susan was released. In that single speck of color was concentrated, for me, all the uncertainty, all the anxiety aroused by having to leave this place—this room, ever more familiar and comforting; these people, so reliable and solicitous; this building, which, although not guaranteed to prevent the return of Susan's assailant, was still safer than the world out there, where we'd have no protection at all. Where would we go? What would we do? How would we get home? Yet the little questions could be just as daunting: Was there enough gas in the tank, or would we have to find a station right away in the thick of rush hour traffic? Did we even have a map of the city? Should we try to find a hotel before nightfall? These were the things that ended up on my list. I couldn't expect Susan to help me with them, and I couldn't see myself managing them on my own. Feeling defeated in advance by such trivialities made me dread walking out the door.

Claire visited us often. She'd begun by bringing all of our things from the guest bedroom in St.-Geoirs. She spent eight hours with us during the first deposition and another three during the second. When Philippe drove our rental car into town, she made the trip too, in her green Mercedes station wagon, so they could go back together. She was the best friend we had in those dark days.

She was fair (fair-skinned and fair-haired), as well as sure of her views, both features inviting wordplay on the name Claire. She loved ancient Greek, which she taught in a high school, and despite being raised in a culture owing so much to Rome, detested Latin, a contrarian trait I found endearing. For some reason, in every memory I have of her she wears a capacious smock, which rendered her already imposing person even more so. At a moment when we were in such need of strong allies, we could appreciate her self-assertive presence. Except, perhaps, for the time when, forgetting about Susan's fractured trachea, she sat on the corner of her hospital bed and lit up a Marlboro.

Once, when she was phoning Philippe from our room, I overheard her say, "Just write your text." That he had a publisher's deadline wasn't surprising, but it reminded me—as when, phoning Susan's parents, I'd thought of commuters in Denver—that the world at large was just going about its business. Not that Philippe was unaffected by Susan's attack. To judge by this call, he was having trouble concentrating. Maybe he felt bad, too, about leaving us almost entirely in Claire's hands.

It was better that way, though. Philippe was a man of few words. Why such people choose a profession that consists essentially in producing words—teaching, writing, lecturing—is beyond me, and I happen to be one of them. But Philippe was extreme, about as far removed as possible from the gregarious man of letters whose natural milieu is the academic reception or the staged gathering of self-important intellectuals in Paris or New York. This was one of the things I'd always liked about him. Yet it left him poorly equipped for these altered circumstances, which called for someone more outgoing, more demonstrative. On the day he brought the car in, he came up to the room for a visit and, standing by Susan's bed, had nothing to say. The burden of the conversation fell on her. They ended up talking about some Latin phrase from Marguerite Yourcenar's *Memoirs of Hadrian*, which she'd been reading before the attack.

Then he and I took the elevator down to the hospital café while Claire stayed with Susan. I believe this was Claire's idea. She may have sensed that Susan and I needed a break from each other, or at least that we should start practicing separation of a normal, everyday variety. Perhaps she suspected as well that changing conversational partners could provide some airtime for neglected or unstated feelings.

What they called a café was a cramped space entirely laminated in linoleum, Formica, and plastic, a spectacle of garish rectangularity accentuated by the buzzing of fluorescent lights and ambient chitchat. It set my nerves even more on edge. Philippe and I ordered espressos and sat facing each other. Conversation languished. I felt compelled to say something. I stammered a sentence or two about Susan's ordeal and then shut up, mortified by words that seemed as conventional and cheap as the décor. Mostly I looked away, now and then back at him. I was very fond of Philippe's uncommonly round, clean-shaven face, his baldness, the intensity of the gaze from behind his glasses, his pensiveness, his occasional throaty smoker's laugh. But things had changed. We were now face to face and far outside the context of all our previous interactions. His silence made me wonder if I'd overestimated the personal connection between us, and, for that matter, what it was I'd expected or hoped for from him. That he take the initiative to ask about me? This was the first time I'd been away from Susan and in the company of someone I'd known from before. Maybe that's why it was also the first time I recall feeling the need for a witness of my own.

When I called my brother, Jim, from Grenoble, he couldn't believe the story I told him. He said if he'd known he would've taken the first flight out of New York—but that the information conveyed to him made it sound like there was no real cause for concern. "Do you want me to come over?" he asked. "Yes. No. I don't know. I can't say how much longer we'll be here. Let me think about it."

There was no doubt in my mind that I bore some responsibility for this misunderstanding. In talking with Susan's parents, I'd downplayed her injuries to some degree and denied she'd been raped. But I could also imagine how, in the retelling by Susan's mother, Martha, the story might have become hazier and even a bit upbeat. Her tone was certainly lively when Susan, on the phone from her hospital bed, spoke with her for the first time since the attack. Martha was so glad, she said, that Susan had a private room. She emphasized the role played by Susan's brother, Don, who had mentioned the situation to a colleague, the brother of Dr. Stahl, who had then called the hospital from Denver. She went on enthusiastically and at length about this, and in particular about the benefit to Don's self-esteem, with hardly a word for Susan herself during the entire call.

Martha had a knack for meeting misfortune with a combination of blatant avoidance and forced cheerfulness. You could say it was a strategy for survival, if seen against the background of her personal history and the history of her poor immigrant family from a desolate town in northern Ontario. You could also say that the high rate of depression, alcoholism, and suicide among the males of the family might help to explain why the upward blip in her troubled son's morale took precedence over the well-being of a daughter just recovering from a brutal assault. You could say these things and more. But so what? Her wildly inappropriate and hurtful response to Susan left me too angry to give a damn about explanations. And I wasn't upset only for Susan's sake. I was just beginning to realize how far the support she would need surpassed what one person could provide. This made me infinitely grateful for any and every kindness shown her by others. It also made me mad when somebody thoughtlessly compounded her suffering and forced me to draw on my dwindling reserves to repair the damage. Our world was drastically out of balance: all the help we'd received still seemed like far too little, whereas a single instance of insensitivity was way too much and could overshadow, at least momentarily, everything else.

We had taken an instant liking to Dr. Stahl. To both Dr. Stahls, in fact, but here I mean Catherine. I don't recall and maybe never knew how she became involved in Susan's case. There must have been a formal assignment, but her gentle, soft-spoken manner made us feel as if she was lending a hand out of personal kindness. And like her spouse, Jean-Paul, she was efficient. It was she who, sitting with us, leafed through a professional directory to find a lawyer.

She dialed a number, requested the desired party, and explained the purpose of the call. Then, chuckling, she asked, "Êtes-vous compétent?" The question could mean either "Are you versed in this area of the law?" or "Are you any good?" To judge from her facial expression as she listened to the response, the person on the other end of the line had at least a sense of humor. It also turned out he was qualified. This was Maître Bernard (*Maître* being the title of any lawyer, and Bernard his last name). We hired him, and met him when he came to attend the second deposition.

He was a good-looking man of medium height, dark-haired, tanned, well-dressed, well-groomed, and bearing, in my eyes, an inescapable resemblance to Mario Cuomo. After the deposition, he remained in the room with us to describe his role in both the criminal and civil suits. Although this was all new to us, it was gratifying just to realize, right after Susan had given her testimony to the investigating magistrate, that she could take another kind of action as well, if only by proxy. That the lawyer would help her do even more about what had been done to her.

But Maître Bernard was also there to share some inside information, picking up a narrative thread left dangling ever since the detectives had suggested a forthcoming arrest. As it happened, the suspect was taken into custody just a few hours after Susan had completed the facial composite. Repeatedly interrogated, he denied involvement but kept changing his story. What's more, the gendarmes had searched the house where he lived with his parents, finding his clothes with mud on them and sneakers whose tread matched prints discovered at the bottom of the ravine. A forensic exam revealed fingernail scratches on his legs, an abrasion on his right arm, a lesion on his testicles.

Susan and I had been listening intently when it suddenly occurred to both of us. "Wait! Wait! Where did the exam take place?" "Right here," said Maître Bernard. "In *this* hospital?!" we exclaimed. "He was in *this* hospital?!" "Yes, this one," he replied, puzzled by our outburst. Susan and I looked at each other. Maître Bernard had just arrived on the scene and presumably hadn't been told about our very real fear that Susan's assailant could come looking for her. Should we take the trouble to explain, when everyone in whom we'd confided up to now had dismissed our concern out of hand? I turned back to him, smiled, and enquired, "What happened next?"

The suspect claimed, in the third or fourth version of his story, told the day after the forensic exam, what Susan and I had already heard from the gendarme who took her first deposition—namely, that she had provoked him into having sex with her. But then, further interrogation revealed that he'd attacked her, raped her, forced her into the ravine, beat her and strangled her, then walked home, showered, changed, and had lunch.

We saw Maître Bernard again, at his office, before leaving Grenoble. This time, Susan shared her fear: she worried aloud that the assailant might gain access, through his attorney or some court document, to her whereabouts in the United States. Maître Bernard didn't get it, though, any more than he'd understood that news of the rapist's physical proximity in the hospital could be alarming. The truth was, we knew little if anything about Susan's lawyer, aside from the fact that his wife was copartner in the firm, which seemed to speak in his favor. If indeed he had experience representing victims of sexual assault, he would surely have learned that the upheaval in their inner world radically alters their perception of the world outside. Presumably, "compétence" in this line of jurisprudence required a special adeptness in client relations. Then again, he was a lawyer, not a psychotherapist. His immediate response was a practical one: from now on, for anything having to do with the lawsuits, Susan could list his office address as her own. He also tried to allay her concern by joking that her assailant, a peasant, had never taken a plane in his life and wouldn't even know how to go about it.

Almost in the same breath, he exhorted her to consider her attacker not as a person, not as a man, but as a wild animal. A beast. A lion. My jaw dropped. Was this meant to suggest that rape and attempted murder were a natural disaster, an accident due to Susan's unfortunate proximity, in space and time, to a lethal force of nature? That the same thing could have happened to anybody walking down that road, that her being a woman had nothing to do with it? That she shouldn't take it personally? And how exactly was this supposed to make her feel better? Or was the point to make *him* feel better? As if it were this man's way of stating, "*I'm* not a rapist."

I don't know what he meant and I'm willing to bet he didn't either. But although invoking a lion was weird, it wasn't unlike a more familiar kind of denial, which, instead of relegating predators of women to the animal kingdom, enlists them in the ranks of the insane. Just seven months before Susan's attack, a gunman had entered the École Polytechnique in Montreal and murdered fourteen women. Yet despite his anti-feminist rant, some claimed it had nothing to do with sex or gender, that it was just the act of a deranged individual. And this happens all the time. Portraying gender-based assaults as one-off, purely random occurrences is a convenient way to circumvent any generalization about cultural misogyny, despite the astronomical number of assaults committed every year.

A forensic exam was required of Susan in order to provide evidence for the prosecution of the crime and also, in the civil suit, a means to evaluate damages and determine compensation. There was no way to avoid it. But the arrangements, made without consulting us, were unsettling. Why did they need to transport Susan to another hospital when the exam could just as well have been performed right there at Michallon, where the police had brought her assailant for the same purpose? Hadn't it occurred to anyone that leaving the confines of the hospital before she was even fit to be released could be retraumatizing? Didn't it occur to us to protest?

The day of the exam, as we emerged from the elevator and headed toward the exit doors, I was more high strung than ever. It was a good thing nobody came near us or ventured, say, to tap me on the shoulder from behind. By then my startle response was hardwired and so severe that in the years since then, it has scarcely diminished.

Beyond the doors, we were in no-man's-land. I was pushing Susan in a wheelchair required by hospital regulations. She gripped the arms, her palms sweaty and her face drained of all color.

There was a car waiting for us at curbside. The driver, a young man, was very friendly. As we pulled into traffic he tried to make polite conversation, unaware that this was no easier for us than chatting in Old Provençal. On our first excursion into the external world, I had to think twice when asked a question like "How are you?" or "Do you like Grenoble?" I seemed to have lost the ability to recognize what such inquiries had to do with anything. Either that, or I couldn't quite imagine myself, or Susan, as the person to whom they should be addressed. At any rate, normal conversational rhythm couldn't really accommodate the time it took me to search for an answer. In the end I must have found one, although it was undoubtedly so belated and terse as to appear pretty rude. He gave up.

Alone with my thoughts, I began to wonder. Here we are, Susan and I, riding through an unfamiliar city in a car driven by a man we've never met before. What proof do we have that he's really who he's supposed to be and is driving us where we're supposed to go? I couldn't even remember if someone had taken us down in the elevator, through the lobby, and out the door to ensure we made the right connection. How was this possible? Because of my very vigilance? Maybe I was like those people whose fixation on locking the door as they leave home is never enough to spare them going back to check. Except I couldn't go back. And now we were on our own, with no witnesses, at the mercy of this driver, who may or may not have been trustworthy. I kept a close eye on him, and another on the scenery. I hoped we didn't suddenly find ourselves in some abandoned industrial park or uninhabited countryside. I also thought I must be crazy.

Finally we approached what looked like a hospital. The driver dropped us at the main entrance with instructions about our return to Michallon. As he took off, we noticed that the place was deserted. Not a single person was visible on the grounds or in the parking lot. Entering the building, we saw no one in the lobby, not a soul even at the reception desk. We hadn't forgotten that the next day was Bastille Day. For many people, the weekend had already begun. Yet illness and injury don't take vacations, and you would have expected some sign of activity at an institution like this.

We waited. It was eerie. I yelled "Hello! Anybody there?" Half a minute later I yelled again. Suddenly a woman emerged from behind a partition, puzzled by our presence, as if we'd missed a sign on the door saying *Fermé*.

We stated our business. She placed a call. We took the elevator. I pushed Susan in the wheelchair as we searched the hallways on an upper floor. Aside from the woman downstairs, we still hadn't seen a human being.

At last we found the right room number. On the threshold, I said again, "Hello! Anybody there?" Two doctors materialized. Both men. In white coats. Taciturn and correct. They led us into an examining room.

One of them said to Susan, "Take your clothes off."

"No," she replied.

"I'm sorry, but for this examination you must remove your clothes."

"I don't feel comfortable doing that. Not without a gown or something to put on."

Slightly miffed, they rummaged around and located a johnny. She pulled the curtain, disrobed, put on the gown. I helped her tie it. We'd already made it clear to them that I'd be in attendance throughout. We drew the curtain back and she went to lie on the examining table.

She hurt everywhere. Several times she called to me and I approached the table to comfort or reassure her. Several times, asked to recount some part of the attack, she broke down crying.

It was tempting to blame the doctors, although by now I was upset enough to blame the whole universe. Should I have told myself they were just doing their job, which was hardly a pleasant one? They seemed to overcome their initial stiffness and to show more consideration. They spoke softly, they made sure the gown covered all but the area they were looking at, they worked quickly so as not to prolong Susan's discomfort. Still, I saw no obvious difference between this manner of theirs and mere clinical efficiency. And I couldn't help but wonder why this task hadn't been assigned to women—women like Dr. Stahl. Was there no one in this medical community attending to the special needs of sexual assault victims?

Either Susan was immobilized on her back, as she had been when her attacker threw her down, sat on her, and punched her in the face; or else she had to lie face down, as she was forced to do in the mud of the ravine. The doctors' hands were invasive. And the procedure was like an autopsy, with every single injury being recorded minutely in a report that eventually covered six pages single-spaced: "fracture of the cricoid cartilege with cutaneous ecchymosis (lesion from strangulation)," "subconjunctival hemorrhages of the left eye, located in the superior nasal quadrant as well as the superior and inferior temporal quadrants," "hematoma of the right cheek, measuring 4 cm by 2.5 cm, purple and greenish."

When the doctors had finished, Susan sat up, swiveled, planted her feet on the floor, steadied herself, walked slowly, while leaning on me, behind the curtain, took off her gown, put her clothes back on, and collapsed into the wheelchair. I pushed her back down the corridor, where we took the elevator to the reception area, still deserted. Outside, the same driver was waiting for us. One look was enough to dissuade him from asking how we were doing.

The next day, we had an exit consultation with a staff psychiatrist. We didn't know if she'd communicated with the medical examiners, whose official report would refer to symptoms of deep psychological trauma. But a glance at the hospital file would have made it clear that the case was very serious.

Our main concern was what to do next. Should we change our plane tickets and go home right away? Or should we continue our trip, if only to spend time with friends we'd planned to see before this happened?

Despite what we'd just been through, our frame of mind hadn't yet adjusted to the enormity of it all. Otherwise, I don't see how continuing to travel—how going on as before—could have presented itself as an option. If I could rewind the clock, I'd whisper in my own ear, "Don't even think about it!" Yet the psychiatrist seemed to harbor no doubts. We should resume our trip in order to restore a sense of normalcy to our lives as soon as possible, she said, even suggesting that not to do so could compound the loss we'd already suffered.

We nodded our heads. We didn't know any better.

Susan was released on the 15th of July, a Sunday. The week before, I'd decided not to take my brother up on his offer to fly over from the States, since it was such a long trip and I suspected we'd be gone by the time he arrived in Grenoble. Luckily, our friend Margot, living in London, was able to join us as we made our way from the hospital back out into the world. Cut loose and left entirely to our own devices, we might have felt paralyzed. As it was, actions that used to be automatic had become oddly unfamiliar. Just crossing the parking lot and unlocking the car door was an experiment, and positioning myself in the driver's seat, which millions of people do unthinkingly every day, reminded me of nothing so much as my first attempt to ride a bicycle without training wheels.

Before leaving the area, we returned to St.-Étienne-de-St.-Geoirs—something we would never have done if Claire hadn't organized a farewell lunch at the house. As we headed out of Grenoble, I got used to driving again, but still could barely imagine traveling up the dirt road to the top of the hill, through the gate where the ambulance had stood waiting, and into the courtyard I'd raced across in a panic. Even less could I imagine what Susan was thinking.

We parked the car by the raised stone terrace in front of the house and let the dust settle. Climbing out, we were amazed to see, under the massive old tree in the corner of the courtyard, a spread worthy of Le Cordon Bleu. Platters of charcuterie, an array of cheeses, all sorts of salads, a large bowl heaped with fresh strawberries, and wine. Clearly, Claire had gone out of her way. We climbed the steps to the terrace, where she and Philippe greeted us. The sun was shining. There was a feast to look forward to.

We were about to walk back down to the courtyard when an elderly couple began to come up. We stood aside. Claire introduced us: these were her parents. We said *bonjour* and shook hands. Their posture was remarkably rigid. This could have been chalked up to age if it hadn't extended to their facial expression, which, even as they greeted us, showed no change from the sternness detectable as they climbed the stairs. And the handshake—the handshake was so flaccid and perfunctory as to suggest the fulfillment of a distasteful obligation.

While we were still uncomfortably congregated at the top of the stairs, Claire abruptly stated, for all to hear, that her parents worked with inmates. I wasn't sure what we were supposed to do with this information. It didn't really seem designed to jump-start a stalled conversation. More likely, it was a roundabout way of explaining why her parents were so frigid with us. Working with inmates implied sympathy for inmates, including the one charged with attacking Susan.

All of this took less than sixty seconds. I might never have given it another thought if Susan and I hadn't both been shocked by the sheer, unmistakable hostility. Or if Claire hadn't later confided that her parents were "old communists"—"old" in the sense of longstanding, or unreconstructed, or both. Was this meant to suggest that, in their eyes, we two professors from prestigious private universities in the United States were unlikely to play a commendable role in the class struggle? Especially compared to Susan's assailant, a member of the rural poor and worthy, on that basis alone, of solidarity? Or did it imply that the problem lay simply in our being American, and subject as such to an antipathy common enough among the French in general but more predictably so in those partial to a communist worldview?

They left before lunch, and we never saw them again. We didn't know for sure what had motivated their animosity—but at the same time, it was impossible to accept that there was *nothing* behind it. When your faith in meaning has been so profoundly shaken, you make whatever sense you can of the world, or else your nervous system makes it for you. To us, class consciousness alone wasn't a convincing explanation. The economic status of Claire's parents—owners or co-owners of the substantial property we were visiting, the likes of which Susan and I could only dream of—was as solidly bourgeois as could be. And besides, Claire and Philippe occupied a social stratum in France very much like ours in the United States. No, it had to be at least partly a question of nationality. The malice we perceived in their gaze told us we were outsiders, intruders who'd put a young man in prison and left his family ostracized. If we hadn't come here, this would never have happened.

That Susan was victimized—and victimized because she was a woman—didn't appear to have registered with them. As for the notion that this kind of thing was the fault of outsiders, I couldn't help but wonder if they subscribed to the main Grenoble newspaper, *Le Dauphiné libéré*, which had printed just a few days before, on the second page, an account of two sexual assaults and two subsequent arrests. Although the victims and perpetrators remained anonymous, we knew the first story was about Susan. The second was about a case of aggravated rape that took place in a neighboring village the very day after Susan's attack. Both the victim, a woman, and the assailant, a man, were natives of the area.

There was a woman at lunch whom I'd never met before. This was the person who'd taken care of Susan when the man on the tractor brought her to a farmhouse. Until the ambulance arrived, she'd held Susan's hand, comforted her. A trained nurse, she could foresee the possibility of emergency surgery and made sure Susan didn't drink anything. Lately she'd been taking walks with her young child along the very stretch of road where the ambush occurred. She was shaken, too. She had long black curls, dark eyes, a Greek nose I found remarkable for how it rendered her whole face so lovely. Under less preoccupying circumstances I might have asked myself which mythological figure she most resembled. Philippe was enamored of her first name, Frédérique. "You know," he said to me, smiling, "that was the name of Goethe's lover during his student days in Strasbourg."

There was also a man I didn't know, sitting across from Frédérique, as handsome as she was pretty. I leaned toward Susan and asked, in a whisper, who the guy was over there, the dark-haired, soft-spoken one. She looked at me, surprised, and whispered back, "That's Luc!"

"Who's Luc?"

"The medic!"

It was embarrassing. I'd spent the most harrowing moments of my life with him—and I didn't remember? Although I was terrible with names, it was initially his face that I'd failed to recognize. Searching for an excuse, I told myself that for me, there was no more connection between Luc and the medic than between this idyllic afternoon and the terror of July 4th. Yet for Susan, Luc was continuity. Whether or not he saved her life, her being here now was indissolubly linked to his being there then. She got to know his face very well, since to see it at all, without her contact lenses and with her eyes almost swollen shut, she needed it to be very close to hers—the face of the man who hovered benignly above her where only minutes before another man's face had grimaced with hatred.

We saw Augustin, with his mother, Hélène. He seemed fine. But who knew? He must have seen or heard something that day, after I abruptly ditched him and the soccer ball. In the hospital, Claire told us he was scared it could happen to him, whatever "it" was in his imagination. In order to reassure him that there was *something* you could do, or not do, to save your life, she'd suggested that Susan had made a mistake in telling the man that her friends would come looking for her. I couldn't say if this had produced the desired effect. Nor could I fathom why she told us, since to our ears it could only sound like an exercise in victim-blaming.

Indeed, Claire could be hard to figure. For on the other hand she'd gone to great, thoughtful lengths to organize this unusual gathering. We were all sitting around the table, enjoying the sun from the soothing shade of the tree, eating, drinking, talking, affirming life in the very act of living it, while the reason we were doing this remained unstated the whole time. No one mentioned the attack. No one so much as alluded to it, even when Augustin had gone off to play. Least of all were there any toasts or tributes. The presence of these guests was, in itself, an acknowledgment of Susan's experience, reflected in a solicitous gaze here, a sudden smile there, a comforting hand, and in the voices themselves, so moderate, so restrained as to make of this bucolic *déjeuner* a much more subdued affair than its visual festivity would suggest. As if the reaffirmation of life were showing respect for what it was up against.

Amid all these signs, however, one stood out. That morning, Susan had debated what to wear. The most appropriate thing seemed to be a V-neck tee shirt. She hesitated, because she still had bruises on her upper chest, which the shirt would expose. But then this became the very reason she decided to wear it. The bruises weren't conspicuous, just a yellowish discoloration at the level of the collarbone. Yet these were among the last visible traces of the attack. If she had to conceal them from these people, what would it be like with others? For that matter, what would it be like when all such traces had disappeared, when only stories remained? Would anybody listen?

6 *Going Home*

We ended up driving straight to Paris, where we could have taken our scheduled flight home a few days later. But we pushed the departure back to allow time to see an old friend in Brittany and then make a trip we'd planned to Belle Île, an island just off the coast. No doubt we were mindful of the psychiatrist's advice and thought this would do us some good. Superb views from the cliffs, bracing air, fresh seafood, walks in the sunshine. Not to mention the appeal of setting off for an island, as if leaving the mainland would permit us to step back from what we'd been going through.

We were lucky to get a room in high season. We felt even luckier when, soon after coming ashore, we found a bistro with outdoor tables and an unimpeded view of the sunset over the Atlantic. We had some terrific *moules marinière* with a very cold, crisp white wine. Just like old times.

Then we went back to the hotel and prepared to turn in. We had no plans for the next day aside from exploring the island and looking for something as good as those mussels. And we were tired enough that sleep would probably come by itself. If not, there was always Lexomil (the hospital staff had given us a small supply as a going-away present). Susan dropped off pretty fast. The curtains were closed, the room was pitch dark, all was quiet around us.

A minute or two later I detected something just audible enough to disturb the peace. It picked up gradually, or my ears became more attuned to it, a cushioned but insistent *tock* whose rhythm was subject to puzzling variations. Finally it sounded like footsteps outside our window.

I got up, groped my way over, and drew the curtains aside. In the faint glow of the parking lot lights, I could see the roof of an adjacent section of the hotel directly ahead of me and a few feet below our window sill. To the right, there was another structure at the same level as our own. I could also make out, in front of me, a couple of large metal contraptions that must have been part of the air-conditioning system. Maybe more of these were positioned above us or to the right, and maybe one of them was dripping. Or more than one, which might explain the variations. But there was no hard evidence. And besides, whatever sedative effect the drip hypothesis offered was offset by the realization that anyone wishing to enter our room surreptitiously could make good use of these adjacent structures. We were a thousand kilometers from Grenoble, but I hadn't left my paranoia behind. Thanks to the perverse refusal of the *tock* to cease and desist, I stayed awake until the sun came up.

That day, we had lunch at a place that was fairly upscale. Susan ordered a *crabe tourteau*, native to the waters around us. Her particular specimen claimed the whole plate on which it arrived—and, as if to make a point, extended its claws toward her like the gloves of a heavyweight boxer. This thickly armored thing was so big it might well have earned pride of place in a museum of natural history. The challenge of eating it would have been daunting enough at a picnic table covered in newspaper, with a bib to put on, plenty of elbow room, and companions who expected you to make a mess. In the present venue, it appeared insurmountable. The longer Susan and I stared at the creature, the stronger was our sense that the only way to proceed would be to put her knife and fork aside and request a set of power tools. We summoned the waiter and listened attentively to his instructions. But these were so complicated and demanding as to convince Susan that the crab was bound to win. And it did, returning to the kitchen intact.

Susan's initial amusement at the absurdity of the situation soon gave way to a degree of frustration that made it clear this wasn't about the crab. I began to wonder what we were doing there, anyway, in that restaurant with its stifling decorum, its linen tablecloths and heavy silver and sparkling stemware. What made us think we'd enjoy it? I'd just lost a full night's sleep to the specter of her assailant, and now she'd been brought to tears by this crustacean. The real absurdity lay in our attempt to resume normal life by way of a summer vacation, to carry on as though the nightmare of her attack were already behind us. We tried to recover by going for an afternoon walk in the sun and the sea breeze. But we had to try, and we knew it.

In the evening, we drove to a nearby village and found a café where we could have a quick informal dinner on the patio. Our mood had clearly deteriorated in the past twenty-four hours. We toyed with our food and discussed, distractedly, whether to leave the island earlier than planned.

Suddenly we were airborne, ejected from our seats by a series of ear-piercing claps right behind us. Hearts pounding, we spun around. Firecrackers. Kids with firecrackers. Innocent fun, if a bit rude and a bit late for Bastille Day.

The next morning, we took the ferry for the mainland and drove back to Paris.

We were happy to spend our last night in France with Monique. To the friend in Brittany, an elderly Frenchwoman, we hadn't said a word about the attack. Maybe we weren't sure how she'd react, or maybe we thought that keeping it to ourselves was a way to be normal again. Monique was our age, and a close friend I'd shared an apartment with in graduate school. We would have told her the story even if it hadn't been the only way to explain why we'd shown up unexpectedly at her place in Paris. More than two years later, she would drop everything to keep us company at the trial.

But at the moment, we were also desperate to get home. An early taxi brought us to Roissy, where we had to take a bus some distance from the terminal, walk across the tarmac, and climb a steep staircase to enter the plane. By then, Susan had somehow developed a nosebleed. It was heavy and it wouldn't stop.

One glance at the cramped and chaotic cabin was enough for me to overcome my natural reserve and accost the nearest flight attendant. Skipping the preamble, I told her my wife had recently been assaulted and asked if she could find us better seats. In all the commotion, I wouldn't have been surprised if she'd flatly refused or, at best, tried to placate us with some extra leg room and a free cocktail. Instead, she looked at the chart and then, to my astonishment, directed us to the upper deck, which felt like being ushered through the pearly gates.

I'd never dreamed of what it would be like to fully recline in an airplane. Susan's nosebleed slowly let up, and once we reached altitude she dozed off. I was just preparing to do the same when I woke up to discover I'd already slept for a couple of hours. With no medication. It felt like the first time I'd relaxed since the morning of July 4. What also struck me was how far my experience of the past two weeks had sunk itself into flesh and bone, into muscles and nerves. I was grateful for the relief of a nap but sobered to realize it was relief from the person I'd become. And if that was true for me, how much more so for Susan?

The transatlantic flight suggested that Fate might be turning a kinder countenance in our direction. But the plane scheduled to take us from New York to Hartford was repeatedly delayed. We sat for hours in the gate area, where the plastic chairs, moulded for some species already extinct or yet to come, rivaled in cruelty the airline's propensity to string its passengers along. So spent already, we found that the very effort required to stay awake for the latest update contributed to the likelihood that we'd be sound asleep when they finally announced boarding. I felt as grimy and unkempt as I did before my shower in the hospital, and Susan, either staring into space or dropping off, looked ghostly in the fluorescent light.

We did have the good sense, once this atrocious leg of the journey was behind us, to take a hotel room rather than drive straight home to New Hampshire. Our car was right there in the airport parking lot, but it was late, it was dark, and I could easily have fallen asleep at the wheel. Not that we were happy about it. Although we were dead on our feet, the pull of home had never been stronger, and few places feel less like home than an airport hotel in the middle of the night. Beyond that, the sheer frustration of not being able to get there seemed to distend retroactively the whole time elapsed since we'd left St.-Geoirs. Suddenly I felt as though we'd been on the road not for seven or eight days but for weeks and months, directionless without knowing it, ignorant of what we needed, prolonging a dislocation for which we'd pay an ever more unaffordable price.

It was tempting to blame the psychiatrist. To say to myself, with no little indignation, that she of all people should have known better than to send us off as she did. I needed to hold someone accountable for this aftermath that was just beginning and had already lasted so long, and it was easier to fasten on her than on the true villain, who was completely inaccessible. But of course no one was answerable to us. And there was no one to explain, as I gazed out of the hotel window at acres of asphalt, why we'd been stranded in this soul-deadening landscape. Or to suggest a script for what lay ahead.

I pulled into the driveway and turned the motor off. I don't remember how long we sat there, staring through the windshield.

Our apartment was pleasant enough. It was small but there was plenty of light. The walls had been repainted not long ago, the floors sanded and refinished. It was conveniently located in a neighborhood that couldn't have been safer. Despite the summer heat, the first thing we did after double-locking the door was to lock all the windows on both floors.

Then we did what other people do. We went through the mail, threw some clothes in the washer, made a grocery list.

But to get food I had to leave the apartment. In the nineteen days since Susan's attack, we'd been out of each other's sight on only three occasions, each time for a matter of minutes and with a trustworthy person keeping her company. Here there was nobody to keep her company, even though the threat remained. I mean, we knew perfectly well we were now on the other side of the ocean, just as, in Belle Île, we were far from Grenoble. We knew the chances of Susan's assailant showing up on our doorstep were pretty slim. But it wasn't just about him. Once the tacit trust you need to move about in the world has been violated, not only the memory of the violation but the threat of its recurrence moves with you, wherever you go. This, at least as much as concern about a particular man, is what Susan brought back from France. As did I, vicariously. The abstract awareness that rape happens every day all over the world was no longer abstract. "All over the world" meant right here at home.

Yet we couldn't just remain housebound. And at the same time, in Hanover, New Hampshire, home delivery was little more than an exotic fantasy, something you could get in faraway places like Boston or New York. If we were going to eat, I had to shop.

I doubt, looking back, that fellow shoppers noticed any anomalies in my behavior. At most a certain impatience or irritability, maybe an exaggerated response to loud noises or sudden movements. To spare them the rest, however—to act more or less like a normal person—required an extraordinary effort on my part. I learned some valuable life lessons, such as how to wait calmly while the little old lady in front of you palpates every single cantaloupe. How to practice your deep breathing when the aisle has been blocked by a spirited discussion of turmeric. How to be civil if not friendly at checkout when all you want is to have done with it and get home.

Once there, I craved a nap. It was bad enough being separated. But having to hide, to contain it all in the company of other people, was something I hadn't reckoned with.

Then a colleague and his partner came to stay with us. People our age, friends in good times. After what had happened on our trip, you'd think we might have felt entitled to cancel or postpone or at least revise a plan made before we'd left. How could we be concerned with etiquette at a time like this? Hadn't Belle Île taught us enough about trying to carry on? As in our consultation with the psychiatrist, it seems we'd hardly begun to register the magnitude of what we'd been through. Susan did go so far as to let these people know over the phone that she'd had a traumatic experience in France, hoping, perhaps, that they'd get the hint. But there was no uptake at all.

So they came. They stayed for four days. We devoted ourselves entirely to showing them a good time and must have succeeded since not once did they so much as venture a polite inquiry about France. At rare moments I managed to forget myself and play the game seriously. Much more often, it took all of my strength to feign interest in conventional topics of conversation when the pain I felt was so far removed from it all and yet pressed so hard from just behind the façade. I'd never had to live two such different lives at the same time and couldn't quite believe the human organism was designed to pull it off. In particular there was, dispatched from somewhere in my interior landscape, a more or less uninterrupted readout that demanded as much attention as the interaction going on outside of me. I couldn't help but worry that right when burning issues of career advancement or social status were being discussed, my private ticker tape would compel me, like some guy with Tourette's syndrome, to blurt out, "You horse's ass!" To gag this ruffian for four straight days, while drawing a smile over my anger and resentment, just wore me out. Whenever Susan and I were alone, we did little more than commiserate and sleep.

Not long after sending these people on their way, we received another visit. Headed to see relatives in Ontario, Susan's parents made a detour. We cooked dinner for them the first evening, just as we had for the previous guests.

Martha talked. There was so much to catch up on—news about aunts and uncles, nephews and nieces, cousins (first and second), the neighbors, the neighbors' dog, the pastor and *his* dog. She went on through dinner and all the way to bedtime. Not a word was uttered by her or Bob about Susan's attack, even though Susan had previously phoned to fill them in on it, including the sexual part.

Just before we turned in, as the four of us were gathered in the living room, saying goodnight, Bob handed Susan an envelope marked *Susan* and indicated she should open it right away. Inside was a greeting card. I leaned toward her and saw a printed message ending with the words "And even though you're all grown up, you'll always be my little girl." At the bottom it was signed "love, Dad." Later, we would reflect on the awkwardness of his having delivered this written message while standing right next to her, with me and Martha present, and on the strangeness of its being just from him. At the moment, Susan was so touched she teared up and hugged him. And then, as was only natural, she moved to hug her mother, too. But Martha pushed her away, held her at arm's length with a hand on each shoulder, looked her straight in the face with a forced smile and declared, "From now on we're going to be happy!" Without missing a beat, Susan shot back, "No! I'm not always going to be happy! Sometimes I'm going to be sad, sometimes I'll be angry!" To which Martha, not used to being contradicted, replied, with the selfsame smile, "Oh, of course. I know that."

I have often lacked for nice things to say about my mother-in-law. However, I'll venture this: inadvertently, she did us a favor. Her denial was so blatant as to bring matters into the sharpest possible focus, prompting Susan to say out loud that silence wasn't acceptable—something she and I needed to hear as much as her parents did. I think Susan was also making a promise to herself: having already been choked by her assailant, she wasn't going to submit to social strangulation—by anybody. She wasn't going to die a second death just because people felt uneasy hearing how close she'd come to the first.

This wouldn't make the road ahead any smoother. Who wants to listen to such things? At every step, one or both of us would have to weigh the risks of telling. But at least we'd find out who our real friends were.

In the meantime, something had to change. We couldn't face any more guests. It seemed like the only way to keep our home from being further disrupted was to leave it.

We went to visit my family in upstate New York, on one of the Finger Lakes. My parents, my brothers, their wives. I don't recall how much they knew, only that, after I'd phoned my brother, Jim, from Grenoble, it was a good deal more than Martha had conveyed. On our arrival, Jim gave me a long, tearful hug. Then he embraced Susan but quickly let go, sensing that the physical contact made her uncomfortable.

People were quietly attentive throughout the weekend. No one pressured us to avoid the subject of the attack, or to bring it up, either. Still, I believe they would have liked to do more than just keep us company. They could see for themselves that things were bad. At a restaurant one evening, Susan nervously insisted on sitting where she could not be approached from behind. This was a tactic she would rely on, in public places, for years to come. It served her well. Yet you wouldn't have known it right then, to judge from her pallor, her fidgeting, her haunted eyes. I sat next to her, preoccupied, on edge, afraid of her frailty.

What I remember most clearly is a moment I spent with my father. When I heard him say he was making a trip to the grocery store, I invited myself along. I realized that this might be my only chance to talk with him alone. And there was something I wanted to ask him.

It had to do with a serious accident my mother was in before I was born. With members of her church, including some of her siblings, she was taking a hayride on a flatbed trailer pulled by a tractor. The rear of the trailer had inadequate reflectors and no lights at all, making it risky for use on a road shared by other vehicles, which was where it happened to be. The sun had gone down and the air was misty. With no warning a car ploughed into the trailer at full speed, sending the hayriders into various orbits from which they eventually landed in the road, on the shoulder, or in a field beyond it. This became a central chapter in our family lore. The Hayride Accident.

My mother suffered a broken pelvis. She was in traction for six to eight weeks, depending on who tells the story. But in none of the versions I've ever heard has it been suggested that my father got any work relief. In addition to a full-time job, he had two young children (my brothers, Gary and Jim), for whom responsibility was only partly taken on by church members. And his wife was languishing in the hospital. I wanted to know what it was like for him. He'd had to be there for his spouse. Maybe I could learn from his experience. Maybe he'd even ask about me.

I brought up the story as we drove into town. He was still retelling it when we got to the store, so I waited until we were back in the car on the way home before prompting him to pick up the thread. I finally saw an opening for my question as we approached the house. When he parked the car and switched off the engine, I turned to face him.

"But what was it like for *you*? I mean, what were your feelings? Wasn't it hard?"

"Oh, I was much too busy to pay any attention to my feelings."

Maybe so. But now that he was retired, his children grown, his wife in good health, was he *still* too busy to think about his feelings? And wasn't he struck that this son of his, after all these years, suddenly wanted to know more about his father's experience in the aftermath of the accident? These were questions I didn't really formulate at the moment, taken aback as I was by what happened next. For no sooner had my father closed his case, so to speak, than he opened the car door, climbed out, and walked into the house without so much as a glance back to see if I was following him.

He was a remarkably caring and affectionate father, and not always averse to displays of emotion. As with many men of his generation (including Susan's father), talking about emotion was another matter, lying somewhere between disinclination and lack of practice, and owing perhaps to the limited value of introspection for people whose first decades of life were defined by such external cataclysms as the Great Depression and World War II. Was this why he had nothing to say about his feelings in the wake of the accident? Or should I have taken what he did say at face value? Just accepted that he'd had no time for self-reflection? Even so, how could he miss the cue?

I couldn't accept an explanation based on the differences (in our jobs, in his having children and my not having any), since the obvious basis of the comparison was a man whose wife had been seriously harmed. Was it the nature of the harm, then? Whereas my mother had been badly hurt in an accident, it wasn't an accident that had almost killed Susan. And it wasn't just an assault, either. It was a *sexual* assault. It could be that, as a man, my father felt implicated in this crime just as I did. He might, like me, have found it hard to sort out the guilt or shame you can feel for what other people do. And then there was this, that he never talked to his sons about sex. Maybe it was prudishness, despite his having grown up in a household of considerable worldliness compared to my mother's Christian fundamentalist clan. Maybe it was a suspicion that whatever he said would be understood to reflect his relations with our mother, the only sexual partner he'd ever had, thus opening a window onto forbidden territory. Or in this instance, it could have been that empathizing with me would entail imagining his own wife as a rape victim, a thought unbearable to him.

My mother later confided to me, "You know, Dad felt really bad about what happened to Susan." "Then why," I asked, a bit riled, "didn't he say anything?" A look of apologetic perplexity came over her face. "Well, I don't know." Only when my exasperation had subsided did it occur to me that he hadn't merely refrained from telling me or Susan how her attack affected him, just as he'd kept to himself whatever he'd felt after my mother's accident. As far as I knew, he also hadn't said a word to anybody about how Susan's attack affected me. In hindsight, I couldn't help but wonder if it wasn't some deep-seated notion of masculinity that brought our conversation to a close on that late summer evening. And if, after all, it wasn't the same notion that had led me, in the ambulance, to suddenly lodge the proof of my feelings for Susan in my very ability to contain them.

My father died of heart failure less than a year after Susan's assault. He'd already suffered one heart attack, followed by a stroke that temporarily deprived him of the ability to speak as well as the ability, or the permission, to drive. But while he eventually recovered both his speech and his car keys, there was no question in my mind that he was preoccupied by his own mortality, for which, despite my disappointment, I hope I made due allowance. More than once, alarmed, I'd caught his beautiful blue eyes staring at something that wasn't there for anyone else. As things turned out, this wasn't just the only chance I'd have to talk with him alone that weekend. It was the last chance I'd ever have.

As soon as we got home from seeing my family, we had to move. Moving was nothing new to us. Dartmouth, where Susan taught philosophy, and Princeton, where I taught French, were 350 miles apart. Every year, we had to invent a way to be together. Usually we managed it by way of a sabbatical or a visiting position, with the inevitable dislocation. If not, we commuted. But this time, as I returned to work and Susan went on disability leave, we'd be settling in suburban New Jersey, where we'd never lived for long enough to establish a sense of community. What made it worse was that we also had to vacate our place in New York, where we'd lived very happily while Susan was a postdoctoral fellow and then a visiting faculty member at NYU.

The period in Manhattan, especially the year preceding the attack, had been a romantic one in our young lives. The apartment we sublet from an NYU professor was an unusually spacious one-bedroom on Washington Square with a stunning view of the Arch, a ridiculously affordable piece of luck at what felt like the center of the universe. Although on many days I had to take the train out to Princeton and back, and although, for a time, Susan was flying every week between New England and New York, none of the hassles familiar to commuters and city dwellers ever detracted from the excitement of trysting in Greenwich Village. We worked better there, too. We could escape the isolation and tedium of research by just leaning out the window and taking in the ceaseless street activity. When that wasn't enough, we'd go out to a club.

It was during that year, in late fall or early winter, that Susan came home one day very animated, as if she'd just seen a fantastic exhibit and couldn't wait to tell me about it. I was slow to respond, only half-attentive, the way you are in everyday life when somebody interrupts what you're in the middle of. "Hey," she said, "I'm talking to you!" She'd just seen her gynecologist, who'd advised her that if we were even thinking of having a child we'd better get busy right away. Like her, I was accustomed to following the dictates of a profession that epitomized delayed gratification. But the doctor had insisted: first the kid, then the tenure review. Now I was paying attention. Who would have thought that making a baby could feel so transgressive?

Six months later, when we left for France, we still hadn't conceived. Maybe it was just as well, considering what could have happened to the fetus from the attack. Then, in the fall after we returned, it was hard to believe we'd ever regain our intimacy. So leaving New York wasn't just a matter of losing a life in which we'd thrived together. It also felt like bidding farewell to the future we'd imagined for ourselves.

Leaving Hanover for Princeton, we had six or seven hours of travel ahead of us. We wouldn't get there until after dark. I was driving a rental van while Susan followed me in the car. If we got separated, the plan was for me to pull off and wait. But everything went smoothly all the way to New Jersey.

At the last toll on the Garden State Parkway, I glanced in the rearview mirror and didn't see our car in the line behind me. I checked in the side-view mirrors, over my right shoulder, over my left shoulder, in the rearview mirror again. Still no car. Then I spotted it, the white Honda Civic, up ahead and several lanes away, pulling level with the booth. In front of me were four or five vehicles, none of them moving. There were others on either side, too. I couldn't switch lanes, I was boxed in. When I looked again, Susan was gone. I felt my pulse accelerating. It was all I could do not to lean on the horn. Why wasn't anybody moving? And why did she do that? I was just hoping I'd find her on the other side of the toll plaza.

No such luck. I don't know how many miles went by before I realized I wasn't going to catch up with her on the Parkway. Maybe on Route 1, the last leg of the trip. Or maybe she'd go straight to the apartment. I was scared. I was mad. How could she do this to me? Wasn't it enough to have disappeared in France?

I turned onto the exit ramp and saw her on the shoulder. I pulled up behind, climbed out, walked briskly to the driver's door. It was locked. All the windows were up. It was hard to see inside because of the street lamps and headlights and neon signs reflecting off the glass. It must have been just as hard to see outside, in the dark. Then she recognized me and the glass went down. I was agitated, I wanted an explanation. But she was sobbing. Had already been sobbing. Her shoulders were shaking, her face was blanched and bathed in tears. The words caught in my throat, just as they had in the ambulance. And just as in the ambulance, this was something I hadn't seen before. Even if the darkness and the loneliness and the lostness that had triggered it were all too familiar, it was as if she was just then feeling for the first time the full impact of what had happened two months earlier.

We managed the last twenty miles without further mishap. Past countless malls, service stations, motels, corporate headquarters, monolithic parking garages, acres of manicured lawn—the whole suburban nightscape of late capitalism—determined not to miss the turnoff for Princeton, which looked like all the others.

When I went to unlock the door to the apartment, I was thinking at least the place would smell new, like the one in Hanover. We'd been told by the university housing department that the whole unit would be cleaned and repainted, as was done routinely between tenants. We'd also been assured that the floors, which were dark and dull and all scuffed up, would be sanded and refinished.

But it didn't smell new to me. I flipped on the lights and walked around. The walls still bore the scrapes and smudges and stains left by the previous tenants. The floors were as dark as ever. Dustballs disported themselves in the corners. As I headed back out, the door caught something. I kicked it free in frustration, looked down. A dirty old mat, frayed at the edges. *Welcome!*

Bone-tired, we schlepped a mattress from the truck into the apartment, dropping it on the dining room floor, where we spent the night. First thing in the morning I rolled off the mattress, located a phone jack, and placed a call. Arrangements were made for us to stay in another apartment until ours was ready. We unloaded everything except personal stuff, then left. The other apartment smelled, too. It was the same smell. A smell that would remain, forever after, the olfactory index of our Dark Ages.

To make matters worse, it was the beginning of classes. No sooner did we get our bearings in the new place than I started heading off to work. Susan was alone every weekday, often for many hours at a time. The locks were all in working order but there was no one to talk to and she was afraid to go out by herself, even for a stroll in the neighborhood.

Besides, I wasn't sure the only threats to her safety came from outside. After seeing her so distraught on the highway, I couldn't help wondering if she might harm herself. I didn't really think so—but then I hadn't thought she'd be sexually assaulted and almost murdered while out for a walk in the sunny French countryside. I'd lost faith in inductive reasoning. In this instance, I wasn't even acquainted with the kind of evidence on which it would have to be based. I wasn't a clinician, I didn't know much about the sequelae of sexual assault beyond what I'd learned since July 4. And yet with a little reflection, it wasn't too hard to imagine how someone feeling the pain I'd witnessed on that exit ramp might resort to extreme measures to alleviate it. Especially as it must have seemed to Susan that she was scarcely less forsaken there in the apartment than she'd been in the ravine. Whenever I left for the office, and even more when I returned, I was defenseless against the intrusive thought that the sight she struggled so hard to spare me in France was what would greet me when I opened the door.

As I approached campus each day, I felt none of the excitement the new school year could inspire even in those who'd spent most of their lives in the academic world. What I felt was a dread that exhausted me before I'd so much as glimpsed the wrought-iron bars of FitzRandolph Gate. I was facing weeks and months of a double life I'd barely managed to live for just a few days when we'd had our visitors in Hanover. Weeks and months of having to answer "How are you?" (or worse, "How was your summer?"), knowing I'd just lie because telling the truth was so tactless or so draining. Weeks and months of maintaining a pleasant demeanor in spite of everything, fully aware that at the best of times people found me too reserved or even mistook my reserve for rudeness. Weeks and months of having to care about what mattered to everybody else, of putting aside the shambles my life had become in order to do my job.

Out of sheer necessity, I improvised a survival strategy: before every class, I locked my office door, lay down on the rug, closed my eyes, breathed deeply, and mentally transported myself to anywhere but there. I was running the risk that the department manager, who had keys to all the offices and stored supplies in mine, might suddenly enter and startle us both. Not to mention what she would make of the strange spectacle I offered. But it was a risk I had to take. And then, typically, a few minutes into class, professional training and experience would come to my rescue. There were even times when I became so absorbed in teaching that I momentarily forgot my troubles. As soon as class was over, I returned to the rug.

This might make it sound like I had absolutely nobody to talk to at work. That wasn't true. I was lucky to have colleagues who cared about me. Suzanne, Lionel, André, François. But conversations with them about what had happened in France were both brief and entirely private, and there was obviously nothing they could do to alter the public nature of the workplace. In the first hours after Susan's attack, when life as we knew it had come to a brutal halt, I'd been struck by how other people were carrying on with their business. Now, I was one of them. I had to be one of them, while also leading a life of almost total seclusion with Susan. Every day brought a sense of dislocation.

But the workplace presented more than one challenge. I was a professor of French and did most of my teaching in French. It had been this way for so long I didn't even think about it. Not until that fall semester, when my feeling for the language showed signs of trouble. Clueless as yet about what these signs might imply for the future, I turned to the past, asking myself how I'd ended up in this line of work, which, after all, was what had led us to St.-Geoirs.

Mostly by chance, to begin with. In middle school I found myself enrolled in French rather than Spanish or German. I don't recall whether my parents and I discussed the options or on what basis the decision was made. Maybe I'd heard my friends were taking French. Maybe the choice had to do with my exposure to the language in fifth and sixth grade, when a lady would drop by the classroom once a week to give us a French lesson. She offered us a break from the everyday tedium of school, organizing games of bingo, for example, to teach us numbers (like *quatre-vingts*, the weird word for eighty that was comparable to *four score*, which I'd never seen anywhere outside the Gettysburg Address). I don't think I retained much else from these lessons, except for the sound of French. But I definitely liked the sound. And later, in middle and high school, I had outstanding teachers, adept at both language training and kindling interest in literature and culture.

None of this would have mattered, however, if my predilection hadn't been reinforced by real life. I grew up near the Canadian border, and with my springboard diving team, made frequent trips to compete in Quebec. There I saw firsthand that French wasn't just an academic subject but the very air breathed by millions of people. Once, in a taxi taking us from the competition venue back to our hotel in Quebec City, my coach asked me to ask the driver what it meant, that sign in the shopping center off to the left, the blue neon *Quincaillerie*. I had a pretty good hunch but asked the driver anyway, who just described what they sold (it was a hardware store). A brief exchange, and every bit as trivial as the bingo games in sixth grade. Yet something clicked in that momentary back-and-forth between languages, giving me the exhilarating sense that French was another world into which I could step at will, as in a fairy tale or Star Trek. By the time of my first visit to Paris, in my senior year of high school, I'd learned the language just well enough to appreciate that learning it a lot better could open the door to a whole new universe and even a very different sense of self.

My take on this was favored by the spirit of the late 1960s and early 1970s, when virtually everything was called into question, including, for me, the Christian fundamentalism that had played so large a role in my childhood and adolescence. What now struck me most about the religion was its deep hostility both to this-worldly existence and to all things intellectual. Who could imagine, by contrast, anything more appealing than French culture? The French smoked and drank, they ate well, they liked sex. They had Paris, they had history, they had great literature. It helped, too, that in my senior-year French class, as in countless others across the United States, pride of place on the reading list was reserved for Sartre and Camus. Existentialism—a term from which Camus distanced himself, but I didn't know that then—said you could decide, all on your own, who you were going to be. Teenagers could hardly have asked for a better drug.

So it was that studying French, an activity initiated years earlier on a throw of the dice, had begun to look oddly foreordained. I chose French as my college major, spent my junior year in Paris, and then, heedless of practical considerations, went on to graduate school, studying with Fredric Jameson and Paul de Man at Yale and, for a year, with Philippe and Jean-Luc in Strasbourg. I got a PhD, made it my life's work. Nothing could explain the willingness to embrace such a precarious livelihood except the centrality French had assumed in the image I had of myself.

It came as a shock, therefore, when I resumed teaching after the attack, to realize this was suddenly changing, and at a level so basic as to defy control, as though a severe illness had actually altered my sense of hearing. Things said in the hallway outside my office, little things in which I'd previously taken an informal socio-linguistic interest when I didn't simply ignore them—these things began to bother me, to get on my nerves. A particular way of saying *oui*, high-pitched and with an intake of breath, or the emphatic sounding of a normally silent *e* at the end of a word (like *ridicule*). Of course, these were affectations, rather far removed from the core of the language. More worrisome was how I felt overhearing standard speech, especially when my ear registered the quintessential rhythm and intonation above the words themselves, as in a muted conversation at the end of the corridor—when it registered that sound of French I'd always loved. Now, all too often, I had an allergic reaction.

My thoughts would sometimes revert to Susan's assailant. He had called her a whore (*putain*) and a liar (*menteuse*). When she begged him not to kill her, he had said *il le faut* (it's necessary), as if he was just doing his duty, just following the scenario. Whenever there were words rather than blows, he attacked her in French, with a voice Susan characterized as gestapo-like. Could there be any doubt that my hatred of this rapist and would-be murderer had affected my relationship with his native tongue? The way he'd made me feel about being a man was bad enough. Could I stomach sharing a language with him? I'd spent many years training my speech in accordance with French phonetics. What if, instead of speaking the language, I found myself wanting to spit it?

There was no one I was inclined to talk to about this. How would it have sounded to my colleagues, especially the native speakers? And what could they have been expected to do about it, even the ones who already knew what had happened? I wasn't tempted to bring it up with Susan, either. Compared to what she was going through, it seemed, like most things, trivial.

Sometimes, when I returned from work, my assumption that nothing happened in the course of Susan's dreary days was disproven, seldom for the better. Once, instead of responding to a knock at the door by retreating to the bedroom, she decided to peek through the small plexiglass window at head height. On the other side was a young man, African American. He could see her as well. Although his voice was muffled by the plexiglass, he managed to get across that he was a high school student participating in a fundraising campaign. What he had no way of knowing was that Susan wouldn't have opened the door to a strange man of any race. When I got home hours later, she was still really upset that she'd been unable to explain to him that it wasn't because he was Black.

On another occasion, she'd been on the phone with her parents, wanting to know why none of her relatives, not even her siblings, had called or written. Her parents claimed that everybody had expressed concern to them but hadn't wished to remind her of what had happened. Did they all think she'd forgotten?

As her fear and sadness made way for anger, she was less inclined to let people off the hook. One day she called her brother, Don, from whom she hadn't heard a thing.

"Is this a good time to talk?"

"Sure. I'm just sitting here watching the Broncos' game. How are things?"

"Well, I . . ."

"So! I hear you're on sabbatical. Just loafing, huh?"

"No, actually I'm on a disability leave. I'm recovering from a sexual assault and . . ."

"They scored! The Broncos scored! . . . What were you saying?"

Just when I thought the housing situation would never change, we were instructed to leave. The apartment was needed for someone else. At the place where we should have been living all along, work was in progress but could only be completed if we first moved all of our stuff to the attic. One evening between eight o'clock and midnight I carried everything up two flights. Boxes of books and papers. Clothes. Dishes and pots and pans and utensils. End tables, chairs, desktops, file cabinets. A colossal futon frame. It was unseasonably hot. My tee shirt was soaked.

By then Susan had left. For several weeks she'd spent most of her time just gazing out the window. She was easily spooked by hiccuping pipes and sighing radiators, not to mention doorbells. It was too much for her to move again, this time to a place that wasn't even furnished and where we were likely to be awakened early in the morning by men putting up sheetrock in the next room. She was on her way to Massachusetts to spend some time with Margot. I was amazed she had the courage to drive there on her own. She said that in a car, even by herself, she felt safer.

I dragged the mattress we'd left there up to a bedroom on the second floor. I scavenged a sheet, a blanket, a pillow from the attic. And a cheap gooseneck lamp, which I plugged in next to the mattress. I folded the pillow behind me and leaned back against the wall, with just the cone of light keeping me company. This was home.

Why didn't they say something? The doctors. Somebody. Why didn't they tell us that the beginning wasn't the worst? That you couldn't count on things getting better? That far from following a script to recovery, you'd be lucky just to get through the next day, sometimes even the next hour or the next minute? And that the longer this took to make sense, the less sense it promised to make? They must have known. Somebody had to have known.

7 *Living On*

On the hearth in the living room stood a bright red ceramic pitcher full of dried grasses, like the centerpiece of a still life. When you entered the room, its light always subdued, this spot of vermillion was the first thing to catch your eye.

My mother put the pitcher there just before she and my brother drove back to upstate New York. They'd come down to Princeton for a couple of days to help us settle into the refurbished apartment. They were the doers in my family, always active and undaunted. They hadn't asked if we needed help. They knew we did and just showed up. I was so grateful I couldn't bear to let on that our condition was immune to practical remedies, since this would've been like telling them they were wasting their time. Besides, I didn't understand it myself. In a former existence, I'd have been buoyed to see that at last we had a stable and secure place to live. And this was to say nothing of the added touch, the *objet d'art*, the vivid red vase with the bright blond grasses, framed in the fireplace against a background of smoke-darkened stone, and whose sole purpose was to afford a little pleasure to people who'd forgotten how to feel it.

By then, more than halfway through the fall semester, it seemed that nothing could halt our slide toward an ever grimmer outlook.

I was exhausted by the effort of straddling the widening discrepancy between life in the outside world and the one we were living on our own. At the end of the workday, in the lull before dinner, I'd trek back from the office with scarcely a glance at the glowing kaleidoscope of late autumn leaves, wondering whether, as happened more and more often, I'd find Susan in bed, asleep or prostrate with depression. As winter approached, the diminishing daylight reinforced our sense of isolation.

Not long after our return to the States, we'd sent cards to Claire and Philippe conveying our gratitude and affection. Claire wrote back toward the end of the summer, a two-page letter with a short postscript from Philippe. They were still shaken by what had happened. When another American friend had come to visit, they'd "kept her on a leash" and never let her stray from the house "without a bodyguard."

They were very worried about Jean-Luc's transplant. Philippe was about to leave for a semester at Berkeley, behind in his work and with too much teaching ahead. And the area around St.-Geoirs was suffering from a terrible drought. But Augustin was thriving, Claire said, and she sometimes saw Luc, the medic, who never failed to ask after Susan. Toward us, she sounded warm and solicitous, like the "friend for life" she'd called herself when saying goodbye to Susan after the farewell lunch.

A little later, we talked on the phone, she and I. From this call I retained only one thing, so unexpected and disquieting as to overshadow all else: she'd paid a visit to the assailant's parents, at their request, and spent four hours talking with them. They lived in appalling poverty, she said. They'd been worried about their son but their worry had turned to despair. And now his already infamous crime had completely cut them off from the rest of the village. The scene was deeply affecting, she added—before sensing from my reticence that I might not share her view and might in fact be wondering why she had done this. She promised to explain in a letter.

In the meantime, I had to tell Susan, and couldn't see any way to do it without upsetting her. She was perfectly aware of how an unscrupulous defense lawyer in a rape trial could exploit information about the plaintiff. Who knew what Claire might have told these people? What's more, the atrocity committed against Susan had divided our moral universe starkly in two, and a "friend for life" had no business on the other side. Claire hadn't even bothered to consult us, as if we, and especially Susan, had no say in the matter. The more I thought about this incident, the more it felt like betrayal.

Susan was shocked. Incredulous. Just as I'd expected. Yet sharing her outrage didn't make it any easier for me. As the messenger, I felt as though I myself had inflicted this wound on her, or at least that, since she would never even have met Claire if it weren't for me, I was somehow responsible for Claire's behavior. I resented this sense of responsibility, tying me as it did to the hurtful recklessness of a so-called friend while exposing me to Susan's anger. I didn't like being in the middle, where I was doomed to displease and where the price I paid for it went unrecognized.

Claire's letter never arrived. By mid-December the suspense had become oppressive, so I wrote from both of us to both of them to say that, for want of the promised explanation, we couldn't help but take a dim view of her visit with the assailant's parents. Given our uncertainty about the criminal justice system, what might strike them as paranoia was really, for us, a matter of prudence.

We asked them please not to see these people again until after the trial.

The reply was dated December 31. Claire took the opportunity of New Year's Eve to express her wish that we might soon make a fresh start (*tourner la page*). She then asserted that "Tom's letter reflected a lot of confusion" concerning in particular what she termed "my relations with my distant cousins." Well, I thought to myself, I may have been distressed when I wrote that letter, but I was certainly not confused. And what was this about distant cousins? Before Susan's attack, Claire hadn't even known these people existed. If she'd given it a moment's reflection, she would surely have understood that such wording could only offend us. *Cousins* implied, between her and them, a kind of relation from which we were necessarily excluded, a long-standing blood tie that cast us as outsiders.

It didn't help to learn that she'd consulted Susan's lawyer before visiting the rapist's home. How could she justify this intrusion into the lawyer-client relationship? And what was the lawyer thinking when he not only gave her the green light but offered advice on the conduct of the visit? From there she segued to the shock these poor people would never overcome, their solitude and suffering, and her own compassion for the downtrodden of the earth. She made it clear she intended to retain her "freedom of judgment and feeling," which, to us, was like saying she'd do whatever she pleased and it was no concern of ours. This made it a challenge to credit her protestation of loyalty ("I'm with you, on your side"), or to hear, in her exhortation "KEEP COOL" (just so, in English and capital letters), anything but a note of condescension.

I responded as carefully as I could. But I made no bones about my refusal to adopt some all-embracing view in which the systemic injustice inflicted on people I'd never even met, as grievous as it might be, was balanced against the rape and attempted murder of my wife. Had I been perfectly honest, I would have added that the very detachment required to weigh such incommensurate wrongs at a time like this struck me as spurious at best, and at worst almost obscene for blinding her to the claims of friendship.

Unbeknownst to me, Claire had already begun a new letter of her own, addressed to Susan, most of which involved a lengthy effort to dispel the various misunderstandings she felt had arisen between them, or between her and us. Due to professional obligations, she'd had to put it aside for a couple of weeks, during which my letter reached her. When she resumed writing, the tone had changed, reflecting the loss of whatever hope of reconciliation had inspired the first several pages. Now she was sad, and also angry. She wondered if all the confusion was attributable to a difference in cultural codes. She wondered if perhaps the time just wasn't right for settling these things. Then she'd put the letter aside again, or misplaced it, for two months. Before sending it, she'd scribbled a postscript: "All of these misunderstandings make me so upset. I no longer know what to do. I don't see what else there is to say."

At least there was consensus on one thing, which was the pointlessness of further discussion. We didn't write to Claire, or hear from her, ever again. Years later I would revisit this quarrel, rereading and reflecting on the letters as a way of mourning the loss of our friendship. But right then, it was impossible to look past the contact with her "cousins."

During this period we also encountered, closer to home, some responses to Susan's story that still stand out like garish neon in the dark and often surreal landscape of post-traumatic experience.

They contributed to a growing storehouse of quotations so thoroughly encoded in the black humor of our private lives that we could exchange them in public as effectively as a wink or a nod.

On the way to work early one morning I ran into a colleague outside the building that housed our departments. He was about my age, very smart and—this doesn't always follow—thoughtful. His interests had equipped him to understand the nature of Susan's experience better than most people I knew at the university, and he had listened sympathetically when I told him about it. On this occasion, not long after the day on which I'd imparted the bad news, he smiled very broadly and asked, in the enthusiastic tone of one who hadn't seen an acquaintance since the previous spring, "So, how *are* you?!" I took a moment to scrutinize his expression for some sign that he hadn't entirely forgotten our recent conversation, but in vain. Finding this as awkward for him as for me, I stammered, "Well, not so hot, really. I mean, you know . . . Susan . . . she's recovering from that attack I mentioned. So, you know . . ." To my even greater surprise, the smile didn't fade at all from his face. I'd already begun to feel like one of the last holdouts in *Invasion of the Body Snatchers* when I heard him say, "Oh, right! And how's that going?"

Another time, after attending a public lecture, Susan was approached by a woman we'd known since my arrival at the university more than four years earlier. She had recently learned about the attack from a mutual acquaintance but hadn't yet laid eyes on Susan. Of course, Susan was seldom around, since she felt unsafe just walking down the street and had concerns rather far removed from the professional routine, which happened to be this woman's central preoccupation. Yet as rooted as she was in academic decorum, as wedded to the conventions of scholarly exchange, she was also, like my colleague, a decent, well-meaning person, and it was only fair to give her the benefit of the doubt. Earnestly, she asked Susan, "So what are you working on these days?"

And then there was the guy who lived just up the street, the partner of someone Susan knew from years past and who, despite his medical training, turned out to be a proponent of the Stiff Upper Lip School. Having listened to Susan's story, he'd exhorted her to "buck up" with such Churchillian resoluteness I wanted to hand him a cigar.

But the standout was an eminent philosopher we had over one evening. A generation older than us, he'd remarried not long before and was accompanied by his new wife. From the moment they stepped through the door, it seemed like young love had turned him back into a boy just giddily emerging from the latency period. During the aperitif, the two of them did nothing but flirt. Had we been more disposed to lightheartedness, this might have been entertaining, even charming. Why begrudge them their happiness? But they made no effort to engage with us, their audience, even to venture a simple "So how are you? What have you been up to?" I had barely begun to serve dinner and I was already asking myself why we'd invited them, especially in light of our experience hosting colleagues back in August. Yet I knew very well why we'd invited them. We were desperate. Giving up all hope of social interaction would have amounted to giving up on ourselves.

The flirting continued over dinner. At one point Susan managed to interrupt the performance of this tandem narcissism long enough to start a conversation of sorts. It had to do at first with daily, relatively low-caliber manifestations of sexism. The philosopher's wife (no trophy wife, by the way, but with a serious career of her own) immediately exclaimed, "Oh, I love it when he pinches my ass!" Whereupon they both giggled. But Susan wasn't to be deterred. She'd already faced down her mother. Who were these people compared to her mother? She started to tell them her story.

This put a damper on flirtation. Faces went flaccid, shoulders slumped, eyes were averted, appetites evaporated. No doubt they were wondering why on earth they'd accepted this dinner invitation. The moment of uncontainable impatience arrived when it became clear that Susan's story wasn't over, that it hadn't ended on the day of the attack or the day she was released from the hospital or the day we returned to the States or the day we moved to Princeton—and worse, that it wouldn't be over anytime soon, because those forty-five minutes of hell, instead of receding into the past, had overtaken the present and the future, so that she found herself unable to think or talk about anything else and . . ."But what," broke in the philosopher, exasperated, "what exactly is your problem?"

Today, we all know about triggers. On that occasion, I didn't even have the word at my disposal and wasn't prepared for what happened. No sooner had the philosopher spoken than I was overcome by an upsurge of rage unlike anything I'd felt since July 4 or since hearing Susan's first deposition. I loved Susan and wanted to reach across the table and bestow on this guy a drubbing he'd never forget. But it was also because I loved Susan that I decided, in a split second, not to do it. He was an acquaintance of hers, not mine. She was the one who'd invited him, not me. Anything I did would just make things worse.

But I couldn't just sit there, either. I took advantage of my role as cook and server to get up, turn away from the table, and walk through the swinging door to the kitchen. Alone, I could let loose, sort of. I leaned against the counter, closed my eyes, and imagined myself smashing every plate and glass within reach, ripping cupboard doors from their hinges, heaving a cast iron skillet through the window. This was the only action film I ever starred in. I don't know how long it ran, but it did calm me down a little. At least it purged me of a telltale scowl in favor of the expressionless face with which I normally greeted the world. And now I could trust myself to return to the dining room and serve dessert without dumping it in somebody's lap.

At the same time, I was puzzled by Susan's attitude. She didn't seem mad. Taken aback, yes, when I glanced at her before leaving the room, but not mad. She appeared to have heard the philosopher's question in a different way, as a blunt but genuine inquiry and not just an attempt to shut her up. Still in the kitchen, I could detect voices on the other side of the door, normal voices, a conversation, which meant, it seemed, that she'd taken him at his word and begun to explain. In any case, she stayed and she talked. Whereas I—I got up and walked away.

I walked away in order to avoid shutting him up, which is what I believed he was trying to do to Susan. Whether or not the belief was justified, my immediate reaction suggested that I felt all the more bound to protect her now as I'd failed to do so in France. Why else would I have responded to the philosopher's perceived aggression by wanting to reciprocate it—with my fists?! And how could I have failed to be puzzled by Susan's staying and talking to him, since it meant she didn't need my protection? Maybe what she needed, instead, was protection from the very rage that almost led me to pummel our dinner guest. True, I could at least give myself credit for having afforded her that. Yet I also think that the anger I carried into the kitchen was further fueled by the sense that the alternative I'd chosen amounted to silencing myself.

And I paid a price for it. For two weeks I simmered, composing in my head a letter to this man that was little more than a verbal version of the thrashing I'd been tempted to inflict on him. At moments my feverish apostrophizing reached such a pitch I'd have to give myself facial massages to relieve the pain from a tightly clenched jaw. But I never sent the letter. I never even wrote it.

As irate as I was, I wasn't about to step back and consider whether this was a one-off thing or the sign of a chronic condition. Only later would it become clear to me that even in my calmer moments I never felt fully licensed to speak, especially in Susan's presence. Had I decided, in this instance, to answer the philosopher's question (with words, not fists), I would have had to refer to her in the third person, as if she weren't even in the room. It would have felt like usurping her voice, like silencing her anew, almost like replicating the crime.

Or like stealing her story. Because it was *her* story, no doubt about it. I was just a supporting character. If anyone had suggested that the story was also mine or that I had a story of my own, I might have nodded politely but more likely would have dismissed the notion, since I knew of no language in which to convey the experience of someone in my position. After all, I wasn't the victim. And even if you could say I'd been indirectly victimized, I also felt, as a man, indirectly complicit. Yes, I was a witness. But I was a witness to Susan, not to myself. All of this—this secondariness—I found confusing.

Sometimes I wonder how much the difficulty of defining such a position contributes to mutism among men in general. If you count just one man—husband, lover, father, son, brother, friend—for every woman who's sexually assaulted, there are hundreds of thousands and more likely millions of men whose lives are affected by violence against women every year in the United States alone.[1] Why do we hear from so few of them? Why did it take *me* so long to make myself heard? Are we all too ashamed to admit we've been affected? Too ashamed of what other men have done and of our failure to prevent it? Could it be that in our own lives—including the lives of those who recognize the political nature of sexual assault—something still inclines us to treat it as a private matter? Or is it that, lacking the status of victim, we don't feel entitled to speak? Even if speaking on our own behalf also means speaking in support of the victims themselves?

The matter of entitlement isn't a simple one. And it's hardly confined to these men. There are plenty of other people you seldom hear, or even hear about, except in the clinical literature on secondary trauma.[2] Clinicians themselves, who listen to stories that, whether related to sexual assault or something else, are traumatic to one degree or another. But also first responders like Luc, whose job routinely exposes them to the pain of others. What did Luc do at the end of the day, or in the following days, to cope with the memory of Susan's frightening condition? And then there are the partners of combat veterans—veterans who, in some cases, have been subjected to *both* combat and rape.[3] Their partners aren't the victims. They don't have stories of their own to tell about Iraq or Afghanistan. Yet very many of them have a diagnosis. And I can imagine the philosopher swiveling toward them to ask, "And now *you*? What's *your* problem?"

I was stuck, consumed by my role, the one I'd chosen back on July 4, in the ambulance, when I'd suddenly "snapped to," bottling up my own distress and devoting all of myself to Susan. It had been the right role to assume then and it still seemed like the right one, since instead of getting better, things had gotten worse. Any expectations we may have had based on a conventional notion of convalescence had been dispelled long ago, stranding us in the dark without so much as a promise of light. What would have happened if I'd started listening to myself? What would I have discovered inside, beyond the anger I already found so hard to contain? It wasn't worth the risk—the risk of leaving us both incapacitated with no one to come to the rescue.

Yet while my determination to remain "in character" allowed Susan to concentrate on recovering, her recovery fostered in her the need for something other than this steadfastness of mine. I was standing still, in a sense, so she could move on—and this put us out of sync. At times, what she wanted from me was an emotional openness rather than my customary stoicism and reticence. "You're walled off," she'd say. Probably so. But I was contending as well with the outside world, which, for now, she could afford to ignore. I had to steel myself to get through the teaching, the advising, the committee meetings, all the other routine professional interactions—my job, in sum. I would even have admitted that on more than one occasion I'd felt a modest sense of accomplishment at having simply survived another day at work, thanks to my armor.

So when I heard her say, "You're walled off," it didn't sit well with me. I sensed a disregard of the life I was forced to live away from home, which was indispensable to both of us. And this planted me even more firmly on the defensive, where I already spent so much of my time with her. I was trying my best. I was numbingly tired, which gave to her simple request for communication the cast not only of a criticism but of yet another demand to be met. And then she herself—reclusive, fearful, depressed, often stuttering, completely preoccupied by sexual violence, and angry, too—she wasn't the woman I'd married.

One evening, late, in the bedroom, I said something. I don't recall the exact words. It wasn't meant to be provocative. Just a suggestion that I, too, had reached the end of my rope. That I thought there was, or should be, more to our lives than this nightmare. Susan later claimed I'd told her to stop moping. I can't believe I would have said such a thing. She cried, "Give me one good reason to go on!" I paused. I was thinking I'd better watch what I said next. But I was also too tired and discouraged to make the effort. I replied, in a barely audible voice, "I can't think of any."

Somehow, we kept going. One day, if not one hour, at a time. To bring some life into the apartment, we got two tuxedo kittens, born of a cat taken in by some graduate students we knew. We named the kittens Ella and Sassy, after two of Susan's favorite vocalists, Ella Fitzgerald and Sarah Vaughn.

At night they slept in our bed, which was still just a mattress on the floor. But not before some organized horseplay. I'd ball up a piece of aluminum foil and toss it down the hall, which extended the length of the apartment, from our bedroom to the head of the stairs. The kittens would race after it, tiny claws scratching for purchase against the wood floor. So eager was their pursuit that they often skidded right past the ball and disappeared over the landing in a tangle of black and white fur. Then a paw would curl over the step, and another, and another, until they'd hoisted themselves up and begun trotting back down the hallway toward us. But the temptation was too great: on the return trip, one of them would inevitably bat the ball, just to teach it a lesson, whereupon the mad race would start all over again and bring this blur of kittenhood tumbling into our laps.

We took them to the vet for a general check-up before we'd even acquired a pet carrier. We put them together in a box, a packing box, with a towel spread out at the bottom. They could peek over the sides but couldn't climb out. It was an odd thing to carry into the vet's office, and too big to place anywhere in the waiting room except on the floor. We were leaning over it, keeping the two of them entertained, when a big orange tabby cat walked out of the examining room. Ella and Sassy caught sight of it—and froze. A moment later they were hissing at each other, and after throwing a few jabs and hooks, fell to wrestling so ferociously we had to separate them. At our request, the vet's assistant spirited the tabby away.

Susan and I looked at each other in something like amused disbelief. Did you see that? Are we projecting? Yet why should external threats to life produce this kind of reaction only in humans? Who are we to think we have a monopoly on transference? Here was an allegorical lesson of sorts, almost comforting in its suggestion that when most humans had abandoned us, we could find common ground with other mammals. Susan called it *A Tale of Two Kitties*.

Coincidentally, around the time we welcomed these feisty little creatures into our lives, I began to see a therapist who'd been recommended to me. With Melissa I could cease being a caregiver, or a professor, once a week for fifty minutes. Once a week, with her, I had fifty minutes all to myself. After telling her, in the first session, about Susan's attack, I didn't have to convince her I'd been affected by it. I also didn't need to hide from her what I tried to spare Susan, or keep up the exhausting pretense of my life outside the home.

So we got down to business. Each week I'd round up my gang of demons and head for Melissa's consulting room. Over time, we pulled every one of them aside for interrogation. Early on she called the gang PTSD, which may have been inscrutable to many laypersons back then but certainly helped with the insurance. Yet I would gladly have footed the whole bill just to see the code number for PTSD next to my name. It meant I wasn't alone. It meant I wasn't the only one, even if I never met anybody else whose demons fit the same diagnosis (not counting Susan, who had it much worse than I). It meant that my unremitting sense of failure was due in part to a medical condition. That this wasn't all my fault.

Then Susan, too, started seeing Melissa. Just when I'd begun to catch a glimpse of myself, to stake a speculative claim on some real estate of my own, we were sharing a therapist. Bad idea, on the face of it. But if there was one thing I needed as much as a witness for me, it was another one for Susan. Somebody to share the listening I couldn't manage by myself anymore. And who might help her listen to me, when she was ready. Even today, when so much has changed in our lives, there is no place more significant to us, in a town that boasts of its history and its university, than the little side street where we used to see Melissa.

I went on Prozac, too. For those who need it as desperately as I did, Prozac, like other antidepressants, can take forever to kick in. The effect was so gradual that detecting it would have required something analogous to time-lapse photography. In any case, there was no magical moment when change was suddenly upon me, no breakthrough bathed in celestial light with the lush accompaniment of the string section. Everything was just the same, yet at a slight remove, not unlike what's suggested by descriptions of mindfulness. That was on the good days. But on those days the marginal relief was enough to make me think that at some point we might be able to get on with our lives. I didn't care that the relief was drug-induced.

In the winter, Susan joined a survivors' support group in Philadelphia. The group met once a week, in the evening, downtown. We would drive together from Princeton, then I'd go read in a café. The first time, I went along to make sure we could both find the place. Just inside the door was a waiting area where the group leader came to introduce herself. She invited Susan to follow her. From the sheer habit of clinging to Susan, I fell in behind them. They both stopped and turned, looking at me. The group leader said I was welcome to stay in the waiting area until the meeting was over.

I felt like such a fool. She shouldn't have needed to convey the message: *No men beyond this point*. At the same time, it brought me up short in another way, this novelty of a woman putting me in my place simply because I was a guy. For a second I tasted what it's like for women in a male culture that fences them in with prohibitions, telling them, in effect, *You can't go there* or *You can't do this*. Perhaps I could have sensed it through an effort of the imagination, but not nearly to the same degree. Because this was a bodily, material restraint, a restriction I felt in my flesh. And yet it wasn't personal. I wasn't confined to the waiting area due to my identity as an individual, but due to my membership in a group: men. I was exchangeable, objectified.

If only, I mused, there was some way to impart this salutary feeling to more men, then . . . then what? We'd achieve a better understanding of women? The world would be a better place? I couldn't say. But I remembered that early reality TV show, *Candid Camera*, and thought a good episode might have resulted from filming, during lunch hour, the reaction of suits on Wall Street being whistled at by an all-female construction crew.

Some weeks later, Susan started making the drive to Philadelphia and back on her own. Once, she sang all the way home. Spirituals, like "Deep River," about crossing over to "that promised land, where all is peace." As she sang she cried. But these were tears as much of yearning as of sorrow, unlike the ones she had shed on that dreadful night six months earlier. And as spring unfolded, she showed even more signs of life: she rode the train once a week to New York for a tap dancing lesson, she took self-defense classes, she made a point of phoning a friend every day, she spent hours listening to music. Then again, at times she would still retreat to the bedroom, which reminded us not to put too much faith in conventional story lines of recovery.

In April, at the Take Back the Night march in Princeton, she spoke publicly about her attack for the first time. So did I, as a witness and supporter. Afterward, as we walked home, she said, "Until now, I didn't know this had affected you." Or maybe, "Until now, I didn't know *how* this had affected you." Neither of us remembers for sure. But I suspect it was the former, since I recall being astonished, incredulous, indignant. How could she imagine I'd been unaffected? We were together every single day. We'd been doing couples therapy, where I was anything but walled off. Did she just need me to open up in public? To hear me with other people's ears? Was it a plea to say more in the future? This was a moment that might have brought us closer. Maybe it did, by showing us how far apart we could still feel.

We were on the move again in June. I was on leave for the next year and Susan had to start teaching in September. We went back to our place in Hanover, arriving in a heat wave bound to remind us of the previous year's homecoming, when we'd pulled into the driveway and stared through the windshield at a future we couldn't even begin to picture.

That night, two female PhD students in the Department of Physics at Dartmouth were ax-murdered a block from our house. We learned this from the headline in the next day's local newspaper.

Life went on. As Susan has written: "Students returning for summer term played frisbee and sunned themselves on the green. Dogs chased balls, families shopped along Main Street, kids ate ice cream cones. Alumni back for reunions paused to look at the ever-enticing real estate photos in sidewalk displays. . . . The Dartmouth flag (almost *always* at half-mast, it seems, to mourn the death of some former trustee or emeritus faculty member or wealthy alumnus) remained at full mast (until a day or so later)."[4]

Both the victims and the perpetrator were Black, and Ethiopian (the perpetrator motivated, it was said, by having been spurned as a suitor). As Susan has also suggested, this seemed to make it easier for people to think it didn't really happen "here." Not to "us." But it did happen here, to Trhas Berhe and Selamawit Tsehaye.

Five days later, my father died. Harry was his name, although everyone called him Bud or Buddy.

I appreciated the chance to pay tribute to him at the memorial service near his home at Keuka Lake. I especially liked sharing anecdotes about his boyhood, a time when I could imagine him carefree and mischievous, long before his face had been creased by the cares of working and parenting and homeowning. I loved that he'd done stuff he'd never have allowed his sons to do, like hopping freight trains in the rail yard behind his house, riding them for miles, then hopping other trains back home. Countless times I'd asked him, as children do, to tell me the same story all over again, the one about the golf shot he'd hit from that rail yard, a picture-perfect six iron that sent the ball sailing right over his house, across the street, and through a neighbor's bedroom window. I smiled as I recounted how he'd sneak into his father's jazz gigs, make his way to the front row and, in plain view of the musicians, suck ostentatiously on a lemon until the trumpet players couldn't go on—then slip away as his father, the pianist and band leader, wondered what the heck was wrong with the horns.

After the service I went off by myself to the top of a hill overlooking the lake. Everything had changed, yet everything looked the same. I also noticed that, except for the narrow strip of water, what I had before me could have been the landscape of St.-Geoirs. It was like the painting I seemed to have stepped into almost a year before while waiting for Susan to come back. There was the same patchwork of rolling hills, of contrasting greens overarched by a vibrant blue. The same stillness, the same silence. Enough to remind me that the anniversary of the attack was just two weeks away.

About the past year, too, I could have said that the world looked the same and had changed completely. What I couldn't actually see was the difference. It lay behind my eyes, informing all they took in while remaining, itself, invisible. As though what you require to know where you are, where you've been, where you're going, is the one thing you can't get hold of. As though you can only live on by backing into your future, fingers crossed.

8 *The Trial*

One day in July, a year after the attack, we found a large envelope from Susan's lawyer in our mailbox. Inside was a cover letter with several enclosures: a psychiatric evaluation of her assailant; a notification sent to the lawyer, along with the evaluation, by the chief investigating magistrate; and the lawyer's reply to the magistrate.

Psychiatrists had concluded that the assailant presented symptoms of schizophrenic psychosis, was not competent to stand trial, and had been in a state of insanity at the time of the act. What this last finding meant, under Article 64 of the French Penal Code, was that no crime or offense had been committed (*il n'y a ni crime ni délit*). In other words, the man who had raped and attempted to kill Susan would not be tried in a court of law, would not be brought to justice. He would be confined to a psychiatric institution for a term to be decided solely by medical authorities.

We hadn't seen this coming. Just two weeks after the attack, a team of psychiatrists had reported that the subject showed no mental abnormality, was competent to stand trial, and had not been insane at the time of the act. For a whole year, we had assumed that an insanity plea had been ruled out and that at some point a trial would take place. What's more, everything favored a conviction:

the material evidence gathered by the *gendarmerie*, the assailant's confession, the facial composite, the forensic exams, and not least of all Susan's depositions, which made it clear that her attacker knew very well what he was doing.

In his letter to the magistrate, Susan's lawyer, Maître Bernard, pointed out that this *contre-expertise* offered no proof of insanity at the time of the act and that it failed to consider whether certain of the subject's current symptoms might have arisen from the very heavy diet of antipsychotic medication prescribed in the wake of his attack on a prison guard. He noted the possibility of simulation, along with the assailant's use of such timeworn tactics as insisting he couldn't remember a thing and claiming his confession had been obtained under police pressure. Maître Bernard emphasized as well Susan's continued suffering, which would only be aggravated if her assailant were not brought to trial. He then formally requested, on her behalf, another *contre-expertise*.

What made this even harder was the distance. Susan's fate (the word is not too strong) was being decided far away by complete strangers. There were long, unexplained delays, as between the second psychiatric evaluation (May 21) and our notification (July 15)—delays that left us feeling as if whatever was going on over there, we'd be the last to find out. And there was the sense, which we'd first had in the hospital, that we exercised little if any control over the master narrative being assembled by a criminal justice system we barely understood. Deciphering the highly coded documents they sent us and following the labyrinthine syntax of judicial procedure was like trying to learn a new language without benefit of either dictionary or grammar.

In her reply to Maître Bernard, Susan highlighted numerous errors in the report's summary of the event. And she asked questions: When it came to the assailant's state of mind at the time of the attack, shouldn't consideration be given to the testimony of the only eyewitness (her)? Why was the second evaluation deemed more authoritative than the first when the first dated from so much closer to the event? Might there be a conflict of interest insofar as the second evaluation was conducted by the very psychiatrists under whose supervision the assailant had been placed (unbeknownst to us) almost a year before? Should she write directly to the chief investigating magistrate about her concerns?

A month passed.

She wrote again, this time to the investigating magistrate. She reiterated much of what she had said to her lawyer but added a few items that might otherwise have escaped the magistrate's attention. It wasn't just that the assailant had resorted to the usual tactics of disavowal while nevertheless undermining his claim to amnesia by mentioning "the woman screaming in the ravine." He had also tried to portray himself as the victim, dwelling on his personal problems (his father's alcoholism, his uncle's suicide, the death of his cow, Maggy), lamenting that "nobody will ever understand me," complaining about his oppression by prison authorities. Meanwhile, Susan had been unable to resume her work for a full year after the attack, which put her professional future at risk. She confronted every day a psychological trauma that seriously tested relations with her husband, her family, and her friends. She was facing substantial unreimbursed medical bills with a reduced salary. Her interest was not in revenge but in seeing that this man, just twenty-six years old, was kept in a place where he couldn't inflict on anyone else the horror she'd experienced.

Another month passed.

At that time of year, it's true, half of France was on vacation and the other half was thinking about it. This could have explained why Susan's letters seemed to disappear into a black hole. But there was ample room for fretful speculation. I wondered if the lawyer or the judge or both of them were rolling their eyes, taking Susan for a pushy American, a customer feeling as entitled in legal as in other affairs, sticking her nose into matters in which they, the lawyer and the judge, had spent years acquiring expertise. "Just trust us," I could imagine them saying. Maybe, on the other hand, they saw her queries as an inconvenient one-off thing best parried through bureaucratic inertia. Maybe they really viewed her as an unusual case, a feisty young philosopher who was raising some rather basic questions about the law—questions to which the answers would just have to wait. Then again, perhaps the lawyer and the judge were both on vacation. Or at least thinking about it.

Another large envelope arrived on October 3. Familiar with delays and the sluggish pace of transatlantic mail, we weren't surprised to see that the most recent *contre-expertise* dated from August 1 and the cover letter from September 23.

This third evaluation concluded that the subject had suffered from a psychological disturbance capable of affecting his judgment and the control of his actions, but that one could not attest categorically to insanity at the time of the act as codified in Article 64. Citing an amendment to the article, it suggested that, in the event of a trial, evidence of pre-existing psychotic tendencies should be taken into account in determining both the sentence and its implementation.

We might have breathed a sigh of relief were it not for Maître Bernard's cover letter, which stated that this evaluation, in conjunction with the others, sent the ball back into the court's court.

Far from resolving the issue of whether the case should be brought to trial, the doctors had saddled judicial authorities with a very difficult decision. No date was given for the decision itself.

By then we'd moved to Lyme, a quintessential New England town with a white-steepled Congregational church, a general store, a post office, an inn or two, an elementary school, a village green with bandstand and memorial cannon, and a cemetery with tombstones dating from the 1700s. About a mile from the green stood an old Cape undergoing renovation. The owner gave us a break on rent since only some parts of the house were habitable and rebuilding the others meant construction noise every weekday. We enjoyed getting to know the carpenter, who'd spent his whole life in that area of the state ("New Hampshah") and was happy to fill us in on what we'd missed. The house faced west, toward Post Pond, just a stone's throw away. Thanks to a wall of large windows, the main room on that side, a very spacious kitchen where we spent much of our time, was set aglow every evening by the sun above the far shore and its reflection off the water (or, in winter, off the ice).

There were also fields around the house where we could go for outings with the two Dalmatian puppies we'd acquired. Like the kittens, they were black and white. Like the kittens, Ella and Sassy, they were named for jazz stars, Max Roach and Dexter Gordon. Like the kittens, they were recruited as allies against gloom—but also as protection for Susan.

I had tried to persuade her that one Dalmatian would do. We both got a kick out of visiting the breeder's place in New Jersey, where we no sooner opened the car doors than a dozen yelping, polka-dotted canines descended on us in a state of riotous ecstasy. But I'd grown up with dogs, and this spectacle gave me pause, especially when we learned that the leader of the polka-dot gang happened to be the sire of the litter we were looking at, a rather porcine and clearly hyperactive specimen called Pinky. Equally alarming, we'd seen *Slaves of New York*, the film starring Bernadette Peters, in which the role of her unruly pet was played by Pinky's own father, a dog named, perversely, Docile.

Experience would teach us to never again make an important existential decision on purely aesthetic grounds (the appeal of black and white, in this instance, or of pet symmetry), and to do our research before admitting a new animal into the household. For the time being, though, Max and Dexter were just part of the picture we tried to draw for ourselves, a picture we hoped would bear more than a passing resemblance to normal life. Susan went back to work in the fall. She taught, she advised, she interacted with colleagues. I stayed home most of the time, attempting to put my sabbatical to good use. When she returned from campus we'd take the dogs for a romp, then have a leisurely dinner together as the sun went down over the pond. Sometimes we'd have people over. We even made new friends. As always with us, the housing was temporary, since we had to go back to Princeton the following year. But aside from the studio in Manhattan, this was the only place that had ever felt like home.

All the same, I ask myself: Is this picture too rosy? Or does it just seem that way because I'd become so suspicious of change for the better? It's true that people who met us then would never have guessed what an ordeal we'd been through. Even I, today, knowing as well the trials and tribulations that lay ahead—even I am kind of astonished by how far we'd come. It was enough to make me think that my post-traumatic skepticism about stories of recovery had created a series of expectations no less conventional than the ones it dismissed. And to remind me that such moments of astonishment can arise wherever two or more very different narrative lines happen to intersect—as when, in the hospital in Grenoble, less than three days after being left for dead at the bottom of a ravine, Susan studiously prepared for the deposition she had to give the next morning. Or when, scarcely a year later, as part of her return to full-time work, she stood before a packed auditorium, introducing Ronald Dworkin, the eminent legal scholar, with a poise and eloquence that could not have contrasted more with the nervousness and stuttering she had suffered from so shortly before. Recently, I saw this performance again, on YouTube. And I was no less astonished.

Hovering like a leaden cloud bank in the background of this picture was, however, our prolonged uncertainty about happenings overseas. In March, well over a year and a half after the attack, we flew to Paris and took the train to Grenoble. We needed to do something, to find out what was going on. We'd made an appointment with Maître Bernard, saying it would be helpful to talk with him in person. He greeted us with his customary charm, then asked, "Why are you here?" We explained our worries, only to be met with a look of incredulity. He assured us that the case was proceeding normally and that there was absolutely no reason for us to have gone to the trouble of making this trip. Maybe it was to give the trip some purpose in his own eyes that he took us on a tour of the Palais de Justice, including the Salle des Assises, the majestic courtroom where, he pointed out, Julien Sorel's trial had been set in Stendhal's *Le Rouge et le Noir*. If there was to be a trial of Susan's assailant, it would also take place in this room.

In May, he notified us that the case had been formally referred to the Cour d'Assises (circuit court), where the accused would be tried for rape and attempted murder.

In late October, when we were back in Princeton, where I'd resumed teaching and Susan was on sabbatical, he wrote to tell us we had a trial date: November 9, 9:30 in the morning, Salle des Assises.

But the relief we'd been waiting so long to feel gave way to alarm and even outrage as we read further. Maître Bernard had tried to push the trial date back because of the short notice—and because he wouldn't be in France on November 9. He then explained why judicial authorities refused to change the date. He also made it clear that he had no intention of rescheduling whatever trip it was he had planned. Every time we read, in disbelief, the phrase "je serai loin de France" ("I'll be far from France"), I felt like telling him it would never be far enough for us and that he should just keep on going. We had a trial, to be sure. But Susan also had a lawyer who couldn't be bothered showing up for it.

He'd engaged a trusted, experienced colleague, Maître Leclair, to take his place, and conveyed to us at some length what we needed to know about the proceedings. Still, we were upset enough that later, after the criminal trial, Susan wrote to Leclair to ask if he'd also represent her in the civil suit. In other words, she tried to fire Bernard. We were certainly aware that this put Leclair in an awkward position, and I strongly suspected as well that such a move would go against the grain of how things were done in France—a suspicion later confirmed by a French colleague of mine, André, who remarked that the arrangement Bernard had come up with wasn't so unusual, gently adding, "You shouldn't have done that." But these considerations simply couldn't rival, at the time, our sensitivity to anything that looked or felt like betrayal. And it made no difference to us when we learned that Bernard was traveling to Israel with Laurent Fabius. So what if, in the general order of things, Susan stood lower in the pecking order than a former prime minister? When everything was on the line for her, her lawyer wouldn't be there.

Admittedly, some things worked in her favor. In Bernard's letter, for example, there was one sentence that stood out, the only one underlined in five pages of text: "*You run absolutely no risk of having your word called into question.*" This was welcome reassurance, although the only thing he said by way of explanation was that it had to do with a respect for victims embodied in the procedure itself, and it was hard to believe that the procedure alone prevented defense lawyers in France, like those in the United States, from impugning the integrity of rape victims and the credibility of their testimony.[1] A fuller explanation would have included the circumstances: Susan was wearing jeans, a sweatshirt, and running shoes; she was walking along a country road in broad daylight; and unlike most sexual assaults, in which the perpetrator is already known to the victim, this was a stranger rape, with no complicating prehistory. Not to mention whatever influence may have been attributed to her marital status, her social class, her professional stature, her race (would she have been viewed the same had she been a woman of color?).

We also had a friend in the mayor of Grenoble. Back in March, at the behest of a well-connected colleague of mine—André, again—the mayor had greeted us in his office, saying how sorry he was about the attack and expressing concern for our welfare. When we returned in November, for the trial, we discovered that two of his aids, Christine and Véronique, had been assigned to give us whatever help we needed during our stay. They chauffered us around town, making sure we got where we had to go and keeping us company at a difficult time. We were privileged, although this wasn't something we dwelled on at the moment.

And then, on the morning of November 9, just before the trial began, we were ushered, with Leclair, into the judge's chambers. We hadn't expected this and didn't understand it. Did the judge customarily meet with plaintiffs before a trial? Did he meet with defendants, too? What about Justitia, the Roman goddess of justice, with her blindfold and balanced scales? Even more puzzling, the judge came right out and said to us, "Tout se passera bien" ("Everything will go fine"). How did he know that? It seemed, strangely, that somebody was looking out for Susan.

As we were turning to leave for the courtroom, though, a slightly discordant note was struck by the *avocat général* (public prosecutor), who had been in attendance throughout this meeting with the judge. The *avocat général* was the person who would plead the case in the name of the state, while Susan's lawyer, Leclair, would plead on her behalf. He was a man of about our age, unprepossessing but, as far as we were concerned, on the right side. He looked at Susan with a certain tension in his facial expression and his posture that suggested he had a serious thought to share. He said, "Madame, when this is over, you must forget that it ever happened." For a moment, we were stunned. Then Susan replied, "But Monsieur, this isn't something I can simply forget!" At which point he insisted, "Il le faut" ("It's necessary"), exactly the tough-guy words used by her assailant when she'd begged him not to kill her.

We entered through a side door and found ourselves in the rear of the courtroom. There, behind a railing, were rows of benches divided by a central aisle. We sat on the right, with our friends, Monique and Marie-Victoire, who had come down from Paris. They planned to transcribe as much of the trial as possible.

The room, impressively long and spacious, had ceilings at least thirty feet high. At the front stood a raised semicircular bench with seats for the judge and the jurors. On the right were separate benches for the *avocat général* and the plaintiff's lawyer, on the left a bench for the defense attorney and, behind it, additional seating. The whole thing was quite grand, with wood paneling throughout, a parquet floor, and a carpet leading to the witness stand at the very center of the room. The ceiling was indescribably ornate, with a large sculpted shield bearing the word *LEX*, held aloft by Justitia and Prudentia. Plenty of light streamed in from the high windows. There were chandeliers, too.

Suddenly attention was focused on a door behind the defense attorney's bench. Through it came four gendarmes surrounding a handcuffed man whose features I couldn't quite make out but who bore no resemblance to my image of the assailant. Scarcely had he entered the room than a loud cry went up to our left, an agonized moan from a woman I hadn't even noticed before. Immediately the judge bellowed, "I will tolerate no displays in this courtroom! I know who you are!"

We'd been warned—by Leclair or Bernard—to expect something like this. We'd been told that the defense attorney was also a coach. He had probably coached the assailant before the second psychiatric evaluation, and had just as probably coached the assailant's mother on how to influence the jurors. Next to her was a man of her age, whom I took to be the father. Here, then, were the people Claire had visited, the "cousins" she had spent four hours talking to. I couldn't really fault them for the outburst. But sitting just a few feet away, I involuntarily clenched, as if to guard against any contact between us. The aisle might as well have been electrified.

Here, too, toward the front of the room, was their son, the assailant. He was scrawny. He moved slowly, seemed uncertain of himself. Not the stealthy, murderous brute I had in mind. A waif, almost. Clearly, prison and medication had taken a toll. Susan leaned toward me and whispered, "He looks nothing like before."

We watched jury selection. The jurors numbered nine, not twelve. The defense could recuse five people, the prosecution four. They both used their quota. It was puzzling: each time I heard "Je récuse," I told myself there was some kind of informed calcluation going on, but in only one or two cases could I even guess what it might be. In the end there were six women and three men. They took seats to one side or the other of the judge.

The trial began with a reading of the indictment. Then the judge turned to the accused and said, "Tell us about your life." Most of this we'd heard, or read, before: the rudimentary schooling, the military service, the uncle's suicide, various jobs, then unemployment. He didn't go out much. His buddies liked to drink but he wasn't into it. He was depressed.

After this desultory exchange, the defense called a series of witnesses who knew something about the defendant's background. They were all in their sixties or seventies and lived in St.-Geoirs or nearby. They all spoke of a family turned in on itself, with a history of psychiatric illness, domestic violence, and alcoholism. The picture was unrelievedly grim. Yet it was also hard to avoid the impression that at least two of these witnesses had, like the accused and his mother, been coached by the defense attorney, concluding their testimony with none too subtle suggestions that the young man couldn't be held responsible.

It became especially clear that the court was still dithering about Article 64—about the insanity plea—when the next witnesses were called: three psychiatrists, one from each of the teams responsible for the evaluations we'd already seen. And then a fourth, who had produced an *expertise* in September that nobody had even told us about. At any point, these witnesses could be interrupted by questions or comments from the judge, the defense attorney, the *avocat général*, or Leclair. It wasn't easy to follow all of this, although the odds seemed to favor skepticism about the plea. The fourth psychiatrist went so far as to claim that being held legally accountable for his actions would foster the psychological rehabilitation of the accused and thus was in his own interest—an unforeseen argument made so compellingly that even the judge sat up and took notice.

Still, by lunchtime recess our nerves would have been seriously frayed if we hadn't retained, like a talisman, the memory of the judge assuring us, "Everything will go fine." Somehow, it also helped to watch Leclair, standing at the bar of a neighborhood café in the lawyer's traditional black robe and white jabot (having temporarily removed his wig, however), prepare for his impending oration by savoring a draft beer.

The afternoon session began with testimony from the chief of the local *gendarmerie*. He talked about the *reconstitution*, an investigative procedure through which the police reconstruct a crime by visiting the scene itself with the accused and with witnesses, including, if she is still alive—and at her option—the victim. Maître Bernard had explained this to us while we were still in the hospital. We found the idea of Susan's participation to be nothing short of preposterous (wondering, at the same time, why *any* victim would consent to such an exercise). She made it abundantly clear that she wasn't going anywhere near the assailant or the ravine. But in connection with this procedure, the gendarme observed what could only make defense counsel squirm: the accused had manifested an accurate memory of the site and, with the police, had pieced together the different stages of the attack.

Then the judge instructed an officer of the court to bring out, for the jurors' edification, photographs of Susan taken shortly after the crime. Assembled in a small album, they were passed from one juror to the next. A hush fell over the whole courtroom, as if the judge had declared a moment of silence. I had also taken a few photos of Susan when we were in the hospital, at her suggestion, just in case anybody ever questioned the severity of her trauma. We probably still have those photos somewhere. But she never asked to see them and I don't remember what I did with them. Now, though, as the jurors leafed through the album, I couldn't help watching their faces, evincing various degrees of discomfiture.

The lull was broken when the defendant's younger brother was called to the witness stand. He lived on his own, worked as a mason, appeared so well-adjusted as to suggest he'd fallen far from the tree. The family had always been reclusive, he observed. They never went out and never had anybody over. He knew his brother was devastated by their uncle's suicide, that things weren't going well for him. He was tense, closed off, he ran long distances at night just to calm his nerves. Yet the witness noticed nothing unusual on the evening of July 4. When he heard about the crime, he told himself it couldn't have been his brother (echoing, in this way, the reaction of people at the farmhouse where Susan was rescued, all of whom expressed the belief that "it couldn't have been anyone from around here").

The last official witness was the father, who walked and talked like a broken man. He barely scraped a living out of his farm, he told the court, and had been under treatment since the arrest. He, too, knew the uncle's death had been hard on his son. His wife told him something was wrong. But he never expected anything like this. Never.

At the judge's discretion, Susan and I were invited to speak. He asked us to walk to the center of the room. Addressing Susan first, he requested that she recount the morning of July 4 and describe her life in the aftermath.

With the depositions, she'd been able to consult notes, take her time relating the event, and review what she'd said before concluding. Not now. Not here. Here she was on the spot, in the very middle of this huge courtroom, in front of the judge and jurors, the attorneys, the clerks and spectators and, not least, the man who had tried to kill her. With no notes and in a language not her own, she had to get across what took place and what she'd been dealing with ever since.

At the end, looking straight at the judge and jurors, she said, "J'ai de la chance d'avoir Tom comme mari. Ce n'est pas facile de vivre avec une femme traumatisée" ("I'm lucky to have Tom as a husband. It's not easy living with a traumatized woman"). I was speechless, just when it was my turn to speak. Why was it that, as during the Take Back the Night march, these intimate things we needed so badly to hear came out only, or at least most audibly, in public? The moment passed quickly but, as at the march, it was clear how both hearing and healing could depend on the presence of third persons, of a community.

I told the court about finding Susan unrecognizable in the ambulance, about my fear for her life, about her incapacitating depression. I also mentioned that we'd been trying to conceive a child, which, since the attack, had been beyond us. No doubt I did this in part for the benefit of a middle-aged female juror whose demeanor throughout the trial had caught my attention, suggesting sympathy, at Susan's expense, for the mother of the defendant.

Thanking us, the judge turned to the defendant and invited him to make a statement, which Marie-Victoire, sitting next to us, wrote down.

"It's too much!" he began. "When I see this person, when I look at the photos, I want to kill myself. I committed this outrageous act and I regret it. I'm guilty. But look at the state I'm in. I'll be sick for the rest of my life, medicated for the rest of my life. What I'm going through right now is really hard. I think I can see my way out but you need to give me a chance."

It remained to be seen, as the trial moved to its conclusion, what his chances would be once Susan's lawyer had spoken. Only when Leclair began his plea did I fully sense how long we'd needed *someone*—someone besides Susan or me—to take up the burden of telling this story. His detailed account of the attack allowed no one to look away from its horrific violence. The attack had lasted forty-five minutes, he reminded the court, and included four separate murder attempts. The plaintiff had been called a whore and been told, when she begged the assailant not to kill her, "It's necessary." He stressed that Susan was the only victim in this matter and spared no effort in depicting its disastrous impact on her life.

He had carefully reviewed the defendant's biography. Admittedly, the defendant had faced some difficulties in life. He was also timid and withdrawn; at times he became aggressive.

Yet if the personal problems constantly belabored in his self-descriptions were enough to generate such horrible acts, then, observed Leclair, "three-quarters of the population would be rapists and killers" (I don't know how he arrived at this figure, although it was enough to make you look around). Moreover, the second psychiatric report offered no support for its conclusion that the defendant was insane at the time of the act. An "impulse" didn't explain a calculated sexual assault and attempted murder extending over forty-five minutes. The court should keep in mind as well, he insisted, that the co-author of this report, who had testified earlier that day, openly admitted that he'd conducted the evaluation without having even looked at the file.

Leclair discussed the material and medical evidence. One by one, he went through the stories concocted by the assailant to cover himself, along with the lies told to police. He could not avoid, he said, feeling indignant at the audacity required to claim that confession of the crime was "extorted." He highlighted the selective nature of the defendant's purported "amnesia," recalling how good his memory had been at the time of the *reconstitution*. "In short," he concluded, "the defendant has fallen into his own trap."

The plea was so thorough and compelling that the *avocat général* could do little more than state his agreement with it. He did point out, referring to the forensic report, that "the pressure on the hyoid bone [in the neck] establishes the intent to kill," and stressed the defendant's "lucidité et dangerosité." Dismissing the claim of insanity at the time of the act, he demanded that the court reject Article 64. He conceded extenuating circumstances in view of the defendant's current condition and called for a sentence of ten years.

By now, we just wanted to get this over with. We watched as the last speaker, the defense attorney, rose from his bench. He paid tribute to Susan for her courage, her dignity, her concern for the truth, and acknowledged that the facts were not in question (all of this being a far cry, indeed, from the conduct of defense attorneys in many rape trials). The issue, he claimed, had to do with the state of mind of the defendant at the time of the act. But this remark was only the prelude to a rambling, interminable disquisition on the history of psychiatry and the law. I glanced at the *avocat général*, at Leclair, at the judge, all of them considerably older and more experienced than the speaker and in all of whom I detected a whiff of impatience, as if they were listening to a disjointed student presentation at the end of a long day at law school.

Returning finally to the matter at hand, the defense attorney singled out the second psychiatric evaluation, according to which the subject suffered from a latent psychosis. Of course, he conceded, it was difficult to date the origin of the disorder. "But this," he proclaimed, eyeing the jurors and pleading for leniency, "this is what I want you to keep in mind. This image of a volcano. The one experienced by our victim."

Whose victim? *Our* victim? Were we all in this together? Was he folding Susan into his rhetorical embrace? Feeling her pain? As for all of these dime-store metaphors . . . first, Bernard had compared the assailant to an animal, a beast, a lion, and now the defense attorney was telling us he had a volcano inside of him. As if the crime in question were a natural disaster, lying entirely outside the realm of human responsibility.

When the judge and jury returned to the courtroom, all were asked to stand. By a vote of eight to one (who was this one?), the jurors found the defendant guilty of rape and attempted murder.

By a vote of nine to none, they found in favor of extenuating circumstances. The defendant was sentenced to ten years of prison, including time served.

He wasn't the only one who had served time. And who would continue to serve it.

9 *And Now*

We were both crying. Was it happiness? Sadness? Something else? Were we even crying for the same reason? Did it matter?

In her book *Aftermath: Violence and the Remaking of a Self*, Susan describes the moment like this:

> When the verdict was announced—"On the charges of rape and attempted murder, the jury finds the defendant guilty"—I felt an instantaneous physical response: my body was shaking, wracked with sobs, although I didn't feel sad or elated. I didn't really feel anything but a sudden unclenching. I didn't have to keep the story straight. It didn't matter any longer if I got it right. I could let go of the details I'd kept alive in my mind, the narrative I'd remembered, rehearsed, and, finally, delivered to the court. . . . My memory had served me (and the criminal justice system) well. A rapist and would-be murderer had been convicted. Now I could finally let down my guard, get fuzzy about the particulars, leave at least some of the horror behind, consign it to wherever they'd taken and left my clothes, my shoes, my belt, the fingernail scrapings, the hairs, the swabs, the leaves, the twigs, the mud, the blood. Now I could, in a sense, forget what happened to me. Now I could afford to think about it.[1]

I remember well the shaking and the sobbing. Maybe I sensed an unclenching, too. But I didn't realize it had to do with keeping the story straight. The assault had been thoroughly documented, thanks primarily to Susan's written depositions, so it hadn't occurred to me that she'd be worried about getting the account just right in her oral testimony.

By then, too, she had told the story in other public venues: at the Take Back the Night march but also, for example, at her high school alma mater, where she had talked about the role of music in her recovery, thereby helping to save the music program from the budget ax. Yet she makes it clear that her reaction on hearing the verdict had to do with the particular version required by the court, a version that had to be chronologically correct, factually flawless, thorough, and exactly the same every time she told it. It was a real straightjacket of a story, unlike the other versions. And if you include the written depositions, then this was a story she'd been telling for a long while. So no wonder she had come to feel imprisoned by the very narrative she'd so carefully maintained. No wonder that, once its purpose had been served, she felt suddenly free of its clutches.

If I felt anything on my own account, it was relief. Now lifted, the stress we'd been under because of the insanity plea became really palpable. A successful plea would have meant confinement of the assailant in a hospital for the criminally insane, where he would have been removed from all judicial supervision and placed under the sole authority of the very psychiatrists who had supported the plea in the first place. They could have released him whenever they felt like it. And when they did, the chances were good he'd attack someone else. Susan was convinced of it.

But there was more to it than that. To me, even psychiatric confinement would have amounted to acquittal. The only institution we could rely on to uphold the laws so grossly violated in the attack—the criminal justice system—would have ended up colluding with the criminal by upholding just one of those laws, Article 64, according to which there would have been "neither crime nor offense." Susan would have been subjected to a second betrayal that compounded the first by denying that the first had ever taken place. Senselessness would have been sealed forever—not only the senselessness of the attack, but of all the efforts she'd devoted to securing a conviction. What would have been the point of fighting back when the guardians of justice declared that there had been no crime committed to begin with? Why bother to scream if they just turned a deaf ear? Could she have lived with that? Could I?

Maybe that's why I'd been focused on the verdict even more than on her retelling. Because this time, there was a collective body to declare, to say out loud, that she got it right. Like me, the court was a listener—but a listener who could acknowledge both the truth of Susan's account and the reality of her experience with the weight of a whole community backing it up. A witness who commanded attention. The verdict was proof that she had been heard. Proof consigned to the public record, engraved in stone, proof of a story she would never again have to contain.

And it was the verdict, not the sentence, that preoccupied us both. People who have read *Aftermath* or who are otherwise familiar with Susan's story often wonder aloud about the sentence. Ten years? Only ten years?! Including time served? For rape and attempted murder?! We nod, knowing it seems light. But aside from the sentence being completely out of our control, the main issue lay elsewhere. We knew that prison wasn't the answer to systemic violence against women, but of the two alternatives—imprisonment or hospitalization—the first was more likely to serve the purpose Susan had pursued from the outset, which was to prevent this man from harming other women. What mattered most was the verdict.

The bailiff encouraged us to vacate the premises. It was late, and the court still had to initiate proceedings against some men accused of double murder at a highway service area. Susan's case was not alone on the docket. I couldn't help wondering if her assailant had been shown leniency on more than one account: extenuating circumstances, for the record, but maybe institutional backlog, too.

We found ourselves outside the Palais de Justice in the bracing alpine air of Grenoble in November, wondering what to do next. I was standing beside our friend, Marie-Victoire, a historian and an activist engaged in fighting violence against women. Unthinkingly, I said, "You know, maybe someday I could write something about this." She turned to look at me full face, slightly astonished, even a bit *scandalisée*. "But Tom," she replied, "it's not a question of whether you could. You must!"

What this imperative probably meant to me had less to do with writing as a medium than with just speaking out in some way, albeit politically and in a very public sense. I was the partner of a woman who had survived rape and attempted murder. It was incumbent on me to take a stand, not only for her but for other women who had been victims of sexual violence. Whether or not Marie-Victoire had this in mind, I can't quite imagine how else I could have heard it at the time. Or how I could possibly have disagreed.

But hadn't I done enough? I'd stayed. I'd listened. I'd commiserated. I'd supported Susan in every way I could, including the really mundane stuff—shopping and cooking, doing the laundry and paying the bills, servicing the car and mowing the lawn. All the communication with France, especially with the lawyer, went through me, and at home I was often the go-between, conveying her experience to other people. While trying to hold on to my job, I'd played the caregiver's role to the best of my ability, with no script to follow. And now I was supposed to become a political activist? This was like asking an athlete who has just finished the marathon to get ready for the pole vault.

Besides, I couldn't see myself in such a role without the creepy sensation of haranguing people from a soapbox. I'd spent the first fifteen years of my life being preached at by one evangelist or another every Sunday, all year long, and every day of the week during summer camp. I used to watch our Protestant hero, Billy Graham, on TV, a man who with words alone (enhanced, it's true, by the coiffure of a prophet) could lift multitudes from their seats and draw them inexorably toward his oratorical perch. Just before the commercial break, he'd incant, "Jesus says, 'Come unto me'!," flourishing his Holy Bible as hundreds upon hundreds of obedient souls streamed into the embrace of professional handlers. By the time my teenage self had recognized this circus of conformity for what it was, the message to which I'd become allergic had permanently tainted the medium of public speaking. No matter how worthy the cause, I could not take part in such a spectacle. I would have to find another way.

In the meantime, our experience had already exacerbated my congenital reserve. More than ever, I was looking for a break from the world. The world had treated us badly. The world had almost killed my wife, had almost freed her assailant, had left me in a state of depletion from which I couldn't imagine recovering and prone to a cynicism I abhorred. Even if I could have overcome my aversion to the pulpit, I would not have headed back out into the world. What I really wanted was for the world to leave me alone.

Since the spring following her attack, Susan had been moving in the other direction. All of the steps she had taken—joining a survivors' support group, learning self-defense, taking tap dance lessons, calling friends, listening to music, going back to work—had been directed *outward*, as ways to reconnect with the world. The same was true of her speaking and writing, now freed from the constraint of the single Right Story required by law. She could tell her tale according to her own needs, the variable purpose of the telling, the changing nature of her audience. Her influential article "Survival Course" appeared in *The New York Times Magazine* just a few months after the trial.

Unlike her, I didn't have a story. At least that was my premise, which hadn't changed since the day of the attack and which contributed to my withdrawal from the world at least as much as fatigue or aversion to the public spotlight. In this, moreover, I was supported by the surrounding culture. If you took a poll asking people whether a man in my position would be affected by an assault like Susan's, I imagine a majority, possibly a very large majority, would say yes. But if you asked those who were personally acquainted with such a man whether they had ever seriously inquired about his own well-being, I suspect the numbers would be disappointing. There were countless occasions on which somebody could have asked, "And Tom, how are you?" It rarely happened.

This is not to bemoan my personal plight or to suggest that I lived among unkind or uncaring people. Far from it. My concern here is really diagnostic: I want to understand a phenomenon that extends far beyond my own case. And one thing I can say is that the problem I encountered was much less a matter of individuals than of a culture as oblivious to secondary trauma even today as it once was to second-hand smoke. Included in the casualties of this unawareness, as I've noted, are psychotherapists, first responders, and the partners of combat veterans—a group to which one could add, for example, the countless health professionals engaged in battling COVID-19. But the invisibility, the neglected or disregarded suffering of those who don't obviously qualify as victims may be especially pervasive among veterans' spouses—be they, as in most cases, the wives of men, or else the husbands of servicewomen, or same-sex partners—given that the care they provide is so readily relegated to the "women's work" our culture has discounted throughout its history. How many times have we been asked, at sporting events, to "honor our veterans"? By contrast, how often have we been asked to honor their partners? Even more striking, when you consider how far female victims of sexual violence outnumber combat veterans, the male spouses of women who have been raped don't even show up on the clinical radar. It's difficult to avoid the suspicion that this, too, is due to a gender stereotype, according to which *men are not caregivers*.

Yet it is also far too easy to talk about culture as if it were simply out there somewhere, and not at the same time inside of oneself. I think back, again, to that moment in the ambulance, when I resolved to be "a man." What if people's apparent lack of concern resulted from my giving the impression of a guy who had his act together? After all, wasn't that part of the role? Didn't it mean I'd succeeded? Associating strength with masculinity had been automatic enough, since every male has it drilled into him from the beginning. The same applied to self-sacrifice, which was just a corollary of strength. Or was it? It hadn't occurred to me that suppressing a part of myself—containing it, keeping the lid on, shutting it up—may have seemed so right at the time because, due to my sex, I felt defiled and shamed by Susan's assailant. From one angle, self-sacrifice may have looked like stoic duty; from another, it resembled something like penance. Nor had I really grasped that I, too, had been hurt, perhaps because being hurt didn't rhyme with being strong or because, in my shame, the injury wasn't worthy of consideration.

And then there was fear. A fear based, no less than the rest, on a cultural assumption, in this instance a deeply ingrained individualism that told me I couldn't raise my voice without silencing Susan's, that I couldn't add my voice to hers without supplanting rather than complementing it, landing us in a divisive zero-sum competition. I worried that, if I spoke up, the assailant would get us after all, ripping apart what we had sewed so painstakingly back together. I would do anything to avoid that.

At the same time, there was another narrative in progress, another kind of trial going on: my tenure review. The senior faculty of the Department of Romance Languages and Literatures at Princeton had met to consider my candidacy just before we left for the trial of Susan's assailant in Grenoble. I was aware of complicated tensions within the Department and could also see that, among other considerations—such as my not being especially prolific as a scholar—certain colleagues of a traditional stripe were unlikely to express support for this Yale theorist with an enthusiastic note from Jacques Derrida in his file. The vote, recorded and sent on to the administration, was positive but not unanimous. This, I knew, could be the kiss of death.

I have no interest in contributing to the vast and lugubrious anthology of tenure tales. Mine, in the end, was not among the most harrowing. But nobody likes to be judged (or threatened with unemployment), and I liked it all the less as Susan's attack and its aftermath had already dealt my self-esteem a withering blow. This in turn was compounded by the humiliating if not infantilizing secrecy surrounding tenure. My relations with colleagues, including the supportive ones, were falsified by what they knew but couldn't tell me, by the unstated *thing* affecting even the simplest encounter. Going to work meant scrutinizing everyone's behavior on the assumption—erroneous but unavoidable—that it was about me. Did he just avert his eyes? Was her comment disparaging? Why are the staff acting so distant? Am I good enough? Am I smart enough? Am I nice enough? Will I make it?

My file languished. Then one day the chair asked to see me. Well, I thought, whether the news is good or bad, at least the whole thing will be over. Instead, he wondered if I could provide a thirteenth copy of my book (at my expense, as with the other twelve, although this wasn't his fault). It seemed the administration was waffling, in need of a thumb on the scales from some scholar whose identity would, of course, remain strictly confidential. Learning that I still had a chance did not, however, take the edge off feeling insulted by this further delay. For months I'd already stewed, at times infuriated that, once again, as with the judicial authorities in France, our fate—Susan's and mine together—was being unilaterally decided by others. And I was tired. I'd been grinding my teeth. Thin my whole life, I'd gained twenty-five pounds.

The call came on a Saturday morning in late February. As soon as the phone rang I knew what it was. I stared at the receiver as though it had suddenly turned radioactive. Two rings, three. At five I might feel rude. Four seemed reasonable, at worst fashionably late. I picked up. On the line was Lionel, my chair. In the first few seconds I tried to guess the answer from his tone of voice, the way you palpate an envelope at college admissions time. Thick or thin? Yes or no? In or out? Did Lionel, a supporter of mine, sound up or down? He sounded tired. Battle-weary. Oh shit.

I don't remember, verbatim, a word of what he said. The gist was that I'd come through.

There were no fireworks, though, not even a bottle of champagne. For that matter, we hadn't popped any corks when my book on Samuel Beckett had come out—and it's a big deal, your first book. That was in the fall after Susan's attack, around the time we received Claire's infamous letter. The fact was that nothing could compete with the attack. The attack was so momentous as to overshadow everything else, so significant that everything else seemed trivial.

Besides, what had I just done? I'd just played a game of winner loses, securing a job more than 350 miles away from Susan. Not that this was new to us. From the moment we'd gotten together, we'd wondered how to stay together, how it was going to work. We'd been on the move ever since, back and forth, again and again, which was less a solution than its deferral. And when things were rough, when we'd been stretched a little too far, it got contentious: What do you care more about, me or your career? A question always trailing its twin: Where is home?

We did try to celebrate by going to dinner at the fanciest restaurant in town. Susan seemed reserved to me, unable to take pleasure in my achievement. Maybe I just imagined it. Maybe I was projecting. I was as stiff as the starched napkin in my lap and about as talkative as a mannequin. Glancing around at the liveried waiters, the linen tablecloths, the expensive china and silver and stemware, I was reminded of that upscale place in Belle Île where we'd tried to retrieve life as it had been before what happened happened. At least this time there was no crab. But like then, there was no use trying. I was depressed and confused. Feeling unhappy made me angry. Why couldn't I enjoy this? Wasn't I entitled to enjoy it? But I also resented the expectation—my own expectation—that I should be happy. I'd had quite enough of fulfilling expectations.

One evening in late March, we drove into New York to have dinner with Chris and Louise, friends from our halcyon days in Lower Manhattan. They'd invited us to their place to celebrate my tenure.

A glass of wine in hand, Susan, Chris and I stood at one end of the kitchen watching Louise, who was in constant motion between the stove and the fridge and the cupboards and the counters, commenting every step of the way on her elaborate preparations.

When we were seated at the table in the next room, Susan complimented Louise on all the trouble she had gone to, raved about how she'd outdone herself. Louise replied, "Oh, Susan, you're just jealous because Tom got tenure."

It was a strange thing to say, even in jest. We were both startled, even embarrassed, not knowing what to make of it. I could tell Susan was hurt.

She may have been especially susceptible because her article, "Survival Course," had come out that very morning in *The New York Times Magazine*, and these friends, who not only knew of the article but had a copy of it right there in the apartment, hadn't said a word to her, not one word of acknowledgment or congratulation. Did they find the subject of rape too awkward? Were they concerned that it would detract from the celebratory mood? Spoil the party? In any case, Susan's accomplishment had been passed over in silence even before she was subjected to Louise's quip.

I was hoping she'd let it slide, just brush it off, for the sake of the occasion. But I didn't expect she would, and she didn't. There was no way to go back beyond that gratuitous and insulting comment, no way to unring the bell. And I couldn't possibly enjoy myself when I knew Susan was hurting. In no time at all, the dinner became an ordeal, an exercise in forced conviviality.

We left as soon as we could, taking with us this marital time bomb set to go off at the first incautious remark. I can't say for sure whether it came in the stairway or the lobby or as we emerged onto the sidewalk and headed for the car. And I don't remember who uttered it. But I'm certain that in what followed, I said something about wanting to experience, just once, a simple, unalloyed pleasure in this achievement of mine. Just once, a moment in the sun. Something, too, about how we would never be free of the attack. And maybe that I couldn't stand it anymore. All of this fueled, no doubt, by too much alcohol.

By then, Susan couldn't stand anymore of me. She was going to find her own way home. This put a sudden stop to my vociferations. What? Go home alone? She wasn't kidding, though. I practically begged her not to. In those days New York was not a friendly place at night. Penn Station was a long way from where we were, and besides, it was so late there might not be any more trains to Princeton.

She turned and walked away. How could I let her go, after what happened the last time she went for a walk? How could she walk away, knowing the effect it would have on me? I stood at the corner, frozen in place. She headed north, crossed Lafayette, and disappeared down a side street.

I drove home, at a loss. We'd worked so hard to rebuild our lives. The trial was behind us. My tenure review was a thing of the past.

We'd stayed together in spite of everything. But how far had we really come? This felt like the night, long ago, when she'd asked me for a reason to go on and I couldn't think of one—only worse, because it seemed like all of our efforts since then had come to naught.

It didn't help that in just a few days we'd be living apart for the first time since the attack. Susan would be teaching at Dartmouth and had rented a house she didn't even like, in a tiny village where she knew no one and would have only the dogs and cats for company. I could get up there for the summer, but then we would move once more in the fall, back to Princeton, before she moved north yet again, in the winter. That was the plan. To any outside observer, it would have seemed obvious that such constant displacement hardly favored a stable relationship. But this was the bind we'd always been in: the only way to stay together was to remain unsettled. It was as if, at intervals of three or six or nine months, a shock sent everything around us back up in the air. Except that now, togetherness was up there, too.

Susan got back in the early morning hours. I don't recall whether we slept in the same bed or were even talking to each other. At times I think only a journal could help me understand how we got through the next day, the next week, the next several months. But I'd never kept a journal, and even if I had it would shed no new light on a period in which things seemed to be standing still and any changes that might have been afoot would surely have escaped my attention. I guess we were stubborn, refusing to admit defeat and hoping perhaps that time would carry us far enough beyond the nightmare on Lafayette to improve our chances of opening a new chapter.

In the summer, we looked at real estate in the Upper Connecticut Valley, telling ourselves that if we were going to continue going back and forth we might at least try to establish a firm north pole. Susan scanned the local listings after we'd lost faith in some agents who had tried to sell us a remote McMansion. And she found something. The house wasn't much to look at: small, rustic, quirky, with exaggerated eaves suggesting a compromise between chalet and pagoda. The interior was better, with a kitchen opening onto a high-ceilinged living room. But it was the site that had attracted Susan, and that charmed us both, on a hill in Vermont with a panoramic view reaching far over the Connecticut River into the foothills of the White Mountains.

We were strapped but managed to put in an offer, which, underlying all of the tedious transactions that followed, amounted to a promise Susan and I made to each other. Eight years after we'd met and more than three years after her assault, we finally had a place of our own. A home we could always come back to and where we could even imagine having company. That may help to explain what came next, I don't know. If I had all the answers I wouldn't be writing this. But by the end of October, Susan was pregnant.

10 *New Life*

Susan sat propped up in bed. We'd reached the hospital at two in the morning and now it was late afternoon.

She was drained but smiling. The baby was fine. A little early, a little underweight, but perfectly healthy. He'd been allowed a short snuggle on her shoulder before they did the Apgar, just the first of many tests on the long road to the SAT.

Now she had a lobster in her lap.

For months she'd been unable to keep anything down that wasn't colorless, odorless, and tasteless, or close to it. White rice. Mashed potatoes. Skim milk. Oatmeal. I'd made adjustments in my own diet. Salsa, for example, had been banned, since she could pick up the scent just from my skin.

Her doctor had prescribed an anti-nausea medication that was also used as an antipsychotic, with strange side effects. It had worked some of the time, while making her shuffle around the house like a sleepwalker. Sometimes it hadn't worked at all. More than once she'd had to excuse herself in the middle of a class to run to the women's room.

A difficult pregnancy, at a time when I was commuting, unable to be home more than a few days a week.

Our friends Ann and Pi brought the lobster, together with a steak, from a restaurant near the hospital. It was fun watching Susan indulge herself. I could almost taste the butter on her fingertips. But I was otherwise occupied at the moment, with the baby in the crook of my arm, all swaddled up and snoozing under his pale blue beanie. Did the medical personnel even offer us a pink beanie? Or something gender-neutral? I don't know. His was blue.

I gazed down at him in wonderment. Somewhere in all of the literature we'd devoured to prepare for this we must have learned that the birth of a child changes the parents' brains. One effect of the change seemed to be that the baby interested me infinitely more than whatever the latest medical research had to say about my brain. Another was to make me sound just like a parent: Look, the tiny fingers are perfect! And he smells so sweet! Hey, he just smiled! No, no, it wasn't discomfort, I swear. He was smiling! A third effect: I was in no hurry to give up this glassy-eyed bliss and didn't care if I sounded corny.

The record would state that he was born at 10:10 a.m. on 7/7 at the Dartmouth-Hitchcock Medical Center. We had been warned that, according to New Hampshire law, you must name a child by the age of seven. Why the rush? Wasn't parenting enough of a challenge already? I hated to think about what happened to people who just couldn't decide: the sirens, the flashing emergency lights, the crackle of police radios.

Since our unsuspecting son would already be carrying a hyphenated surname, we needed to keep it simple. When the nurse looked up, questioningly, from the form she was filling out, we turned to each other and exclaimed in unison: "Gabriel!" It hadn't been planned this way—the unison, I mean. But *Gabriel* had always hovered at the top of the charts. We liked the sound. We liked the association with an angel who heralds new life.

They let us spend two nights in the hospital. We had a private room with a foldout couch and a TV. On the third day, shortly before we left, I sat on the couch, cradling Gabriel, and tuned into the World Cup. We were lucky: the match being broadcast featured Brazil and the Netherlands, two of the very best teams. I propped Gabriel up so he could watch with me. I wanted him to learn to enjoy *o jogo bonito* (the beautiful game) and to appreciate other countries like a true internationalist. Just before halftime, I looked down to make sure this was sinking in. He was sound asleep.

There's a photo of the three of us, taken on a shaded deck against a sun-drenched background of meadows and woods. I'm seated, in khaki shorts and a red tee shirt, my right arm under the reclining newborn, my left around his midriff. He's snoozing in his light-blue one-piece footie. Behind me and to my left, Susan, in a green shift, is perched on the railing and leaning forward, her head next to mine and her right arm around my shoulders. We're both looking at the camera, smiling contentedly.

The picture was taken at our house in Vermont. Only a few days before, we had sat on the same deck, quietly commemorating the anniversary of the attack. Now we had company. On the evening we brought Gabriel home, we stood out there to enjoy the view while also cooing at him, still beanie-capped. There would come a day when he would no longer wish to be cooed at. For now, we could coo to our hearts' content.

The meadow in front of us sparkled with fireflies. *Lucioles*, in French, from the Latin *lux*, light, as in *Fiat lux*, let there be light. Above us, where the atmosphere was untainted by artificial illumination, the stars scintillated (from the Latin *scintilla*, spark). We could see heat lightning on the horizon. And across the river, in Lyme, where we had lived not long before, they were setting off some impressive fireworks, making up for the rainout on July 4. In Japan, too, they were celebrating. It was the Star Festival, called Tanabata ("evening of the seventh"), beginning on July 7 of the Gregorian calendar. Gabriel's birthday.

I took comfort in the simple fact that Gabriel came *after* the attack. That he would be spared, for years, any awareness of it. And that, whenever he did learn about it, the new chapter he had opened in our lives would have long since forced the previous one to move over and make room. Raising him, taking pleasure in his life, even promised to resurrect a *before* in both Susan and me.

Meanwhile, I got to feed him. Susan had found breastfeeding too painful, despite repeated attempts. By the time the nurse, dismissing her complaints, insisted she make one last effort, Susan was engrossed in the lobster and shot her a look like a laser, prompting a hasty retreat and allowing me to step in with a bottle. In no time at all I was preparing and administering formula like a seasoned veteran. I suppose Gabriel was too young for this to register as an exercise in gender equity. But if memory can't recapture such moments, then what, I ask, was the point of playing him Mozart in utero?

Anyway, I loved this tactile relationship, which I continued to have with him when he was a toddler. Lifting him up and supporting him with my left arm, my right arm, hugging him with both as he wrapped his legs around my waist. Hoisting him onto my shoulders, tickling him in the ribs, squeezing his toes while joking about the importance of separating them every day. Cradling him on one side as, on the other, I propped up the book we were reading and slowly turned the pages.

We read a lot. Every night. Books came into and went out of favor but there were always plenty in reserve. One large-format book about Paris included an elaborate two-page spread depicting French pastries: éclairs, napoleons, cream puffs, raspberry tarts, and more. We would choose one pastry for each grandparent, aunt and uncle, cousin, and close friend, and send them off for delivery the next day.

Dr. Seuss's books figured prominently, as did other classics, from Margaret Wise Brown's *Goodnight Moon* to E.B. White's *Charlotte's Web*. They lightened me up. You can't very well read to a child—or more to the point, you can't read to a child very well—if you're not willing to play the game, to enter into the fictional world of the book and become a child again yourself. Reading with Gabriel revived my imagination, which had suffered from sheer neglect, like a muscle atrophied through disuse. It took me outside of myself.

In future years, we spent a lot of time in the car, like most Americans. Gabriel was strapped into his seat in the back. We talked. One topic we revisited was how the highway department managed to trim the trees on our road in Vermont. For it was one thing to mow back the weeds along the shoulder and quite another to prevent overhanging branches from reducing visibility or even bending over to collide with cars and pickups, not to mention big trucks. How did they do it? We tested various hypotheses, but, in the end, the truth was plain to see. What they did was hire helicopters to fly sideways along the road, just above the telephone poles, and lop off those branches all the way down to the covered bridge at the bottom of the hill. We never saw or heard the helicopters, but that didn't mean a thing. You just had to admire the cleverness of the pilots and the creativity of our highway department.

One day, during a lull as we rolled along, the voice from the back seat suddenly asked, "Is infinity for real?" Susan and I glanced at each other. Where did this come from? And why now, when the birds and the bees weren't even hovering on the horizon? I had just opened my mouth to reply when I recalled hearing a colleague quip that having nothing to say never prevented a professor from talking. True, Susan was also a professor, but she had a formal training I lacked. "You're the philosopher," I said, "you take this one." In keeping with the Socratic method, she sent the ball back to him, inquiring what he meant by "real" and citing helpful examples. She pointed out as well that people held different views on the matter, which didn't seem to bother him in the least, however, perhaps because he was more interested in the chat than in its outcome. Or was he just pulling our leg?

But on another occasion the little guy asked, "Is there such a thing as life after death?" This was harder than the issue of infinity and reality, since it tended to get personal and required a more forthright response. Susan has reminded me that it came up shortly after the death of our cat, Sassy. She and I had both experienced, in childhood, an existential crisis due to the loss of a pet. Yet Gabriel had never evinced the slightest worry about the fate of our Dalmatians. He certainly hadn't objected when we placed one of them, Dexter, in a new home, and he might even have welcomed the disappearance of the other one, Max, who was no less a bred-in-the-bone anarchist than his brother and was always scattering Gabriel's carefully arranged Matchbox cars. No, he was much more attached to the cats; and Sassy's having just passed away made it more than likely that the question was prompted by her. But was it also about him? Or about us?

We suggested that there *was* such a thing as life after death because pets as well as people lived on in the memory of those who had known and loved them. Yet soon thereafter, on reflection, I heard the question in another way, which was indeed about us, about the choice Susan and I had had to make. A question to which Gabriel himself was the answer.

11 *More Trouble*

The night was so dark you could barely see the snowdrifts through the windows. The temperature, already glacial, was still falling. I sensed this might be one of those winters in which the cold grew so severe it would bring tears to your eyes if you just stepped outside—then freeze your fingers to the doorknob as you tried to get back in. Adjusting the thermostat, I wondered whether, like me, the first Europeans to settle in Vermont had had second thoughts.

But we were snug inside. Gabriel, almost eighteen months, was slumbering in his crib. Both of his grandmothers, who had traveled far to see us, were asleep upstairs. The cats were curled up on our bed, while the dog sprawled on the living room floor, occasionally yipping in accompaniment to a muscle spasm or two as he merrily relived the day's misdemeanors in his dreams. Susan and I retired to our room, trying to wind down. It was Christmas Eve.

The phone startled us. It was a bit late for holiday greetings. Who could it be?

Susan answered right away, hoping the ring hadn't woken anyone up. The caller identified himself as a doctor at the hospital in Portland, Oregon, where her brother, Don, had been admitted to the psychiatric unit a few days before. The doctor said their father,

Bob, was with him. Bob had been planning to join us in Vermont but flew to Portland instead when Don made it clear he wasn't doing well.

The strange thing was that the doctor asked Susan to hand the phone to me. This was Bob's idea, he then told me, offering a vaguely worded rationale I would think about later. He went on to say that something had happened after Don's condition appeared to stabilize in the afternoon and a pass was issued allowing him to leave the hospital for a few hours in the company of his father.

They'd gone out to a restaurant, their mood enhanced by the break from hospital routine and by the holiday activity in town. To Bob, Don really did seem to be doing better. Recently so depressed, so unforthcoming, he had become remarkably lively and talkative, which Bob found encouraging. They enjoyed themselves so much their pass had almost expired by the time they finished dinner.

When they got back to the hospital, Bob had a feeling common to many men his age (he was seventy-four): he needed a restroom, quickly. Having earlier noticed one right there in the garage where they'd just parked the car, he excused himself, saying he'd be only a minute and then they'd walk to Don's room together. But on returning to the car he didn't find Don. Just a note.

The doctor didn't say what was in the note. He just reported to me that Bob had hurried over to the railing at the perimeter of the garage, six stories up, and looked down. He said that Bob saw Don lying on the sidewalk. That Don had dived and fractured his skull. That Don was dead.

While I was taking this in, Susan, sitting next to me, wanted to know if it was serious. I nodded. The doctor suggested I put her on so he could have a word with her before she talked with her father. As I handed her the receiver, she asked, "Is he dead?"

“I’m really sorry,” I replied.

“Oh my god! Oh my god!”

I don’t recall if I stayed there to be supportive or left the room to give her privacy. Or both in succession. At some point, feeling a parent’s vulnerability, I checked on Gabriel. But I was peripherally aware the whole time that there was another person in the house, still asleep, who had to be informed and whose life would never be the same.

With Bob still on the line, Susan and I climbed the stairs and kneeled down next to the couch where Martha was spending the night. I was the designated messenger, no better prepared for this than for the call I had made to her and Bob from the hospital in Grenoble. I placed my hand on her shoulder and said softly, “Martha?” She opened her eyes, momentarily disoriented, wondering where she was and what time it could possibly be. When she noticed us both by her side, she sat up, slowly.

I apologized for waking her up, explaining that Bob was on the phone. “He’s with Don’s doctor, at the hospital in Portland.” She nodded, waiting. There was no way to spin this, no way to cushion the impact as I had done when calling from Grenoble about Susan. In just a few seconds she would get the full story from her husband. My job was to tell her the end of it, the worst. “I’m afraid Don has taken his life.”

Her face changed in a flash. But it wasn’t only anguish, or distress, or sadness I saw there. It was something like recognition. Recognition and resignation—defeat at the hands of what she had always feared, the specter of suicide that had carried off other men in her family and had now taken her only son. Her face was shadowed all at once, as if by a mourning veil acquired long ago for just this occasion. “He was such a beautiful boy,” she said.

We stayed there as she took the call. At one point, her voice rising, she asked Bob, "Why did you leave him alone?" Feeling a hand on her arm, she looked up. Susan was shaking her head, whispering no. She was right. Yet it wasn't surprising that Martha wanted to blame. Who wouldn't? Who wouldn't seek an explanation, a cause to go with the effect, some sense to allay the senselessness?

By then it was midnight. My mother, in an adjacent room, was awakened by our voices. I told her what had happened. At Susan's suggestion, I called my therapist, rousing him from a sound sleep, apologizing, explaining, asking him to come over. He drove the ten miles from his place in the dark and the snow and the freezing cold.

It wasn't for me that I'd phoned him. It was for Martha and Susan. Or perhaps for all of us. I suppose it was a kind of communal distress signal. But I don't know what we expected him to do. The best psychiatric training in the world would be of limited avail if, like him, you were unfamiliar with the family and its history. Besides, none of us was feeling very talkative. I think it was his mere willingness to come that made a difference. His willingness to sit with us, to keep us company in our helplessness.

We flew to Denver for the funeral, returning home a week later. The trip was a blur to me except for a few snapshots. Shortly after the service, a number of people were standing idly around the kitchen in Bob and Martha's house when Martha, beaming, exclaimed that she had found a reason to be happy: Don was with the angels! While no one could blame her for seeking solace in religion, no one said a word in response. Everyone looked away, awkwardly. I happened to catch Bob, a skeptic, staring at the floor, unable or unwilling to meet Martha's gaze, which had frozen us all in a peculiar *tableau vivant*.

A day or two later, Don's psychiatrist from the Portland hospital phoned to say he happened to be in the Denver area and asked if he could drop by. A time was arranged. Then we thought about it. Somehow it was hard to believe he just happened to be in the area. This in turn made it hard to believe that his motive was purely humanitarian. Maybe he was there because he knew the family had questions about his conduct on the day of the suicide, in which case a house call was only prudent.

We sat in the living room, a formal room full of fine furniture and usually empty of people. The perimeter was now lined with a profusion of heavily scented flowers from the funeral. We were prepared for the doctor to fill in some blanks. Why had he abruptly discontinued the medication Don had been taking since his admission to the hospital? How did he decide that the improvement in Don's condition wasn't a momentary anomaly or an illusion? What made him think it was safe to allow Don out of the hospital, even briefly? "Well," he replied, "he was with his father!" I can't say for sure if he squirmed while uttering these words, which implied that it was accepted procedure to saddle a seventy-four-year-old with responsibility for a seriously disturbed patient on an outing in a strange city. I do retain the image of him perched, amidst all those flowers, on an elegantly upholstered and obviously uncomfortable chair. When he rose to leave, his story was still trailing loose ends. But it was difficult to dismiss the thought that, for him, it would have served its purpose if it forestalled a malpractice suit.

At home, nothing had changed. There was snow. It was cold. The days were short, the nights interminable. The routine was identical: Susan went back to teaching, Gabriel went back to day care, I went back to my study, on leave for the year.

But the sameness wasn't the same. We'd had a shock. Now would come the pain. I was apprehensive without knowing what to expect. I myself had never been close to Don. For that matter, I wondered if anyone had ever really been close to him. Just before the funeral service, a cousin who knew him well told us he'd found him exceptionally remote even in childhood. Susan mentioned to me that in his high school yearbook he had quoted, next to his photo, a poem called *Invictus*, a kind of hymn to the fortressed self, whose last lines now sounded like an epitaph: "I am the master of my fate / I am the captain of my soul."[1] Once, when Martha had asked him a question, I watched him walk into another room, return a minute later, and mumble, "Yeah." I thought, Is it me? I don't remember Martha being upset. Maybe she was used to it. And there were exceptions. I'd seen him laugh, as he may well have done with Bob during dinner on the last evening of his life. For Gabriel's first Christmas, he'd bought him a toy train, which he had as much fun with as Gabriel did. Yet these moments had been rare, and I couldn't recall a single conversation between us in the nine years I'd known him.

Most of what I knew about him came from stories told me by Susan, stories in which he seldom figured as a sympathetic sibling. I'd also seen for myself how little if any concern he'd shown after her near fatal attack. And for years he'd resisted any acknowledgment, let alone any treatment, of his depression, seemingly oblivious to the effect it had on other people. This made it hard for me to look beyond the wound he'd inflicted on his parents, on his older sister, Mary, and on Susan. How do you mourn a brother toward whom your feelings may have been mixed at best—but who was, after all, your brother? How do you grieve when the cause of death was suicide, which can arouse as much anger as sadness, can bring you back to the *why* as often as the *what if*? And where did I stand in all of this?

I phoned my brother, as I had done from the hospital in Grenoble. He'd had some experience with the aftermath of suicide. Several years earlier, he'd cleaned up the room where the husband of his wife's best friend had placed the tip of a shotgun barrel in his mouth and pulled the trigger. Then he had supported his wife, and together they'd supported her friend, and as time went by it took a very heavy toll. My brother also knew what I'd been through since the assault. He said, "Tom, don't take this on." It was loving advice. But after the call I realized I wasn't sure what it meant. He was deeply fond of Susan and wouldn't have wanted me to bail on her. Did he have her family in mind?

I suppose so. Yet it would have been challenging in any case. More than five years had passed since Susan had been left for dead at the bottom of a ravine. In post-traumatic time, however, five years can seem like a heartbeat. I hadn't forgotten the price she'd paid for the poor support of loved ones in the crucial early months after the attack. And wherever this memory may have been lodged—in my body, my heart, my mind or soul—it was unmistakable in its effects, over which I had little if any control. Recalling the neglect from which Susan had suffered, even as she was now being called upon to support her parents, aroused in me a keen sense of injustice. At the same time, how could I admit feeling indignant or resentful, even to myself? Since when was resentment an appropriate reaction to people who have just suffered catastrophe? Good people. Kind, gentle, well-meaning people. People who nevertheless had proven, on more than a few occasions, remarkably unattuned to their children's needs. If I wasn't sure what to do it was perhaps because, unlike my therapist, I *did* know this family and its history. Then again, like my therapist, I could at least keep Susan company.

In the meantime, I had occasion to reflect about that phone call from the doctor in Portland. What had he said? That Bob suggested he talk to me first because . . . because what? Because, not being a member of the immediate family, I was less vulnerable to the message? It must have been something like that. I was at a remove from it all, and so could better withstand the shock, could register and convey the message with less emotional interference. I'd been put at the center of communication precisely because I was peripheral. And I couldn't help wondering, with a newfound sympathy for the doctor, what it was like to have a job that required you to be, routinely, the bearer of bad news. To be, as I knew from my less frequent experience, just a reliable conduit, ensuring passage without absorption.

It remained to be seen, though, how well I could keep Susan company, given that, for many months before the suicide, my own state of mind had been deteriorating. Unexpectedly so, at a moment when things were looking up for us. We had a healthy, endearing child, a community of friends in Vermont, a house that felt like home. Not only was the criminal trial over, but the civil suit had been settled, too, so that, thanks to Susan's indemnification by the French government, our finances were no longer as precarious. And I didn't have to worry about tenure. All of these happy turns might have been expected to buoy us up in the new time of trouble, and doubtless they helped, even if, in light of the suicide, life's overall intelligibility had seen little improvement. So why was it that I'd been so depressed? Had these changes for the better meant that I could afford to relax, in a sense, and that distressful feelings

I'd suppressed in order to remain a functional human being could begin to emerge? Had I embarked unwittingly on a kind of apprenticeship, one with which Susan was already familiar, an apprenticeship in the pain of healing? I couldn't have answered these questions and wouldn't even have known if they were the right ones to ask. This in itself—this confusion—was a symptom of depressive disorder.

Since I was on sabbatical leave, I spent most weekdays alone in my study. Susan was usually on campus and Gabriel was with our friend Shifra, his day-care provider. There were no distractions except Max, the Dalmatian, who at least gave me an excuse to get out of the house for a walk and some sunshine. My study had a fine view of the snow-covered fields, the forests, the distant mountains, a view often changing with the state of the sky and the time of day. It didn't help. It had no effect on the atmosphere of the study, which was gloomy at best.

So far from my usual workplace, the university, I had nothing to rely on in the way of an institutional raison d'être, a daily justification of my existence. It wouldn't have mattered so much if my scholarship had been progressing. But I was stuck. I had received a fellowship to produce a second book on Beckett, only to realize, as I set to work, that I would never write it. Maybe I'd never write another word. It wasn't a matter of writer's block or of the proverbial post-tenure slump, despite a superficial resemblance. I didn't know what it was. I just knew that from the day of the attack to this leave, the only reason my professional profile had held up was that most of the work to which I owed tenure had been completed before the attack itself. Now, when I thought I'd pursue the same kind of work, I found it impossible. I just didn't, just couldn't, care. Psychiatry characterizes this symptom of depression as a "loss of interest in meaningful activities," although, from the patient's point of view, it could just as well be considered a matter of the activity—in my case, scholarship—losing its meaning. And there was nothing to take the place of the book, not even some short-term project to tide me over. Nothing. It was as though I'd been walking a tightrope toward tenure, had somehow reached the far stanchion, and was just muttering "Phew!" when the whole apparatus collapsed beneath me.

It was alarming. My love affair with France was already in serious jeopardy. To suffer, in addition, such a sweeping disinvestment in scholarship made me wonder how much more of myself I could lose before discovering there was hardly a self left at all. The fade-out wasn't under my control, either. I didn't *choose* to be estranged from France. I didn't *choose* to become indifferent to scholarship. With a little perspective, I might have found a name for this experience. Or if I'd had a name, I might have been able to back away and take a good look at it, even find a place for it in the story of a man whose partner had been raped and beaten and strangled and left for dead in the mud. Was it shame, perhaps? Or despair? I didn't know, since in fact I had no perspective. I was inside the thing. And as for stories, what did I really have to show? The truth was that nothing had happened to me. I was a crimeless victim, as invisible as a spouse as I was as a scholar.

Occasionally I'd be ruminating on my plight, or staring at an empty screen, or watching the wild turkeys that pecked their way lazily across our meadow when I suddenly realized it was time to drive over to Shifra's and pick up Gabriel. This provided a distraction every bit as effective for an adult in the doldrums as did a certain kind of ploy recommended for children in the middle of a tantrum.

"Hey!" you'd say to the little ones, "how about some ice cream?!" Or else, "Hey! Wanna go to the beach?" It worked like magic, or so I was told. Likewise, I'd say to myself, "Hey! Time to go get Gabe!" And as I walked to the car I'd be reminded that it was no longer dark at this hour. Soon we would put March behind us and head for the summer solstice, with its promise of light and warmth and outdoor play.

At moments like these, it didn't escape me that I was a lucky man. Not only did I have a child to love, but I got to spend a lot of time with him. It didn't escape me either that I owed this time to the very profession with which I'd become so disenchanted. Even when teaching, I was able to devote a larger share of my day to child-rearing than could parents in most other lines of work. I suppose I could have patted myself on the back for recognizing long ago, in my choice of a job, that time was infinitely more important than money.

Yet I only had the job because my parents had made it possible for me to go to college, something they'd never had the chance to do. And I only had the lifestyle because American culture had changed since they were my age. Back then, in the 1950s and early 1960s, I would not have been picking up my kid from day care. For one thing, there *was* no day care. For another, this was not a man's responsibility, even if the man was a scholar whose working hours were spent just spinning his wheels. A man's responsibility was to bring home the bacon (or the Spam). As for my wife, I doubt she would have had a career. She would have had her hands full keeping house, raising the children, and baking pineapple upside-down cake for my colleagues, all of them male. On weekdays, after dinner, the family would have gathered in front of the TV to watch *Father Knows Best* or *Leave It to Beaver*.

My mother, Mona, could turn out pineapple upside-down cake with the best of them. She also made no bones about the condition of women. She had always wanted to be a boy. Boys were freer. Boys had more fun. Her brothers had had their pick of extracurricular activities, while she was expected to come straight home from school and wheel the newest of eight siblings (a boy) around the neighborhood in a baby carriage. When she got married, she had done what was expected of her, which was to quit a good secretarial job and become a full-time housewife and mother. That she excelled at both didn't change her view that fulfillment lay as well in getting out of the house and making her own way in the world. Once I, her youngest, had reached my teens, she went back to work. Over the years she reinvented herself as a small business manager, a real estate agent, a commercial artist. She was happy.

Seeing my mother so contentedly engaged in the world, I found it inconceivable that I would end up with a woman lacking similar ambition. For the same reason, I couldn't fathom my mother's own idea of the one who would be best for me, based on the premise that I was too serious. "You know, Tommy," she once remarked, doubtless hoping to lighten me up, "they say it takes sixteen muscles to frown and only four to smile!" I may have smiled then, wondering where she could have unearthed such cutting-edge science. *Reader's Digest*? But although I didn't generally feel all that serious, I had to credit the premise to some extent, since it had been confirmed many times and by multiple sources, including a graduate school professor who regretted to report that Mr. Trezise was "too grimly intense and sober for mainstream classroom teaching." The real trouble began, however, with the conclusion my mother drew from this premise, which was that I needed a carefree, happy-go-lucky girl. At times she would dramatize this by joyfully waving her arms in the air, like Julie Andrews singing "The Sound of Music." To me, the image it evoked looked more like Doris Day in an apron, with a big grin on her face as she twirled a feather duster and reveled in the freedom from thinking. It was the stuff of nightmares, and the best argument I'd ever come across against wedlock.

All of this became null and void as soon as Susan entered the picture. A philosopher! Ergo, not the carefree, happy-go-lucky girl my mother had in mind. Yet she took to Susan from the first, and not only because Susan's sparkling green eyes, and her winsome cheeks, and her dancer's figure, and her warmth and grace made Tommy smile. The smile was certainly nice, suggesting an improvement in her son's outlook, to say nothing of its sheer novelty. But my mother's love was far too spontaneous to weigh conditions or calculate consequences. She just took to Susan. And Susan to her.

What I had learned from my mother's example pertained not only to my mate, however, but also to me. If a woman's place wasn't only in the home, then mine didn't have to be exclusively outside of it. During my year of leave, I was as happy being a dad as I had ever been as a teacher or scholar. Admittedly, I didn't have to shoulder the responsibility imposed on most mothers, since we could afford day care. And the recalibration of gender roles was hardly a simple thing, since I was still a creature of patriarchy, having long been conditioned to think that my value as a man depended in large part on my place in the external world of work. At the time, this meant that the professional paralysis in which I found myself wasn't likely to be alleviated if I remained much longer where I was, tracking turkeys from the solitude of my Vermont study.

But that's what I did. How could Susan face her tenure review the next year, in addition to teaching full-time and caring for a young child, when her commuting spouse was away half the week?

I took another year's leave, this one without pay, feeling occupationally more insubstantial than ever.

Gabriel was a toddler, and a sweet one. But I didn't need a developmental psychologist to tell me that even a child of his age could pick up on a parent's prevailing mood or emotional disposition. And the last thing I wanted was to inflict on him the gloom in which I so often felt myself shrouded. For all I knew, he might be carrying a genetic inheritance to be reckoned with later in life. I didn't want to compound it by bequeathing to him—through my comments on people and things, through the way I looked at him or spoke to Susan, or even through my physical posture—the dreariness that weighed on me. Yet I also didn't know how to proceed when so much of it was unconscious. How could I monitor myself if I wasn't even aware of what my face looked like in repose? I would try. I would do my best. I would keep in mind what my mom had told me about those muscles.

Much of our time over the next year was consumed by tales about the behavior of some colleagues of Susan's, tales I found increasingly difficult to listen to as the behavior grew more treacherous. Susan had made a name for herself in philosophy of law and in innovative work on the relationship between the personal and the philosophical. This work had challenged certain norms of traditional philosophy, helping expand the scope of the discipline to include such topics as sexual violence and the role of narrative in the formation of the self. In doing so, it had generated various degrees of resistance in proponents of the status quo.

Most of her colleagues—not all, but most—were men. They'd been friends of ours, or at least chummy acquaintances, before their smiles turned into frowns, as if the faces so familiar to us had never been anything but masks. Somewhere, Theodor Adorno claims that in psychoanalysis, only the exaggerations are true. Perhaps that also holds for post-traumatic life. It may seem exaggerated to suggest that for me, listening to stories about a few of Susan's colleagues made getting through tenure feel like her surviving the sexual assault. But reduced to its simplest terms, the process unfolding over that year looked to me like an act of aggression being perpetrated while I could only stand by, helpless.

I once let on to a close friend that I, too, was paying a price for this tenure business. I must have assumed that knowing about our past would allow her to infer that it wasn't easy for me to watch a couple of men try to derail Susan's career. And this assumption, reinforced by my being too proud or too shy to come right out and state the case, led me instead to angle for sympathy by casually suggesting that I could use some inpatient psychiatric care. I wasn't serious. In fact, I had no interest in such a thing. My remark was just a clumsy effort to indicate that a little show of concern could go a long way. Something simple like, "Gee, is it that bad?" But I suppose it served me right when our friend took the remark literally and replied, "You might want to wait until Susan is through tenure."

Yet there was, throughout this spell of visible darkness—during which I often wondered how, after the attack and the suicide, Susan could sustain a third blow, like the denial of tenure, not to mention how we would cope with it as a couple—there was the possibility of a favorable outcome, thanks not only to the excellence of Susan's file but also to women in the profession who recognized the importance of her work and were determined to maintain the integrity of institutional standards. They reminded me of how, on that summer day in France, as I kept my vigil at the crossroads, I wished there was someone to watch over Susan, someone like the benevolent deity I used to believe in. But in this instance there was no question of a former belief or a higher power. What made the difference was women with the courage to stand and speak. Much like Susan herself. Who got tenure.

Long before the decision was announced, I had sensed that, even if it turned out in Susan's favor, my pleasure and relief would remain strangely hypothetical, less like feelings in the present than possibilities reserved for a future in which this nightmare would have begun to fade. No doubt this had much to do with my preexisting depression, a state that often left normal emotions in abeyance for lack of a self to register them. Although I will never forget the exuberance with which, immediately after a phone call from the dean of the faculty, Susan announced that she'd been granted tenure—to the robust cheers of all those gathered at our house—it was Susan who had drawn my attention to Primo Levi's eloquent summary of "conditional" emotion in the statement, "If I still had my former sensitivity . . . this would be an extremely moving moment."[2]

12 *A Glimpse of Gabe*

The happy chapter beginning with Gabe overlapped for a time with some of our darkest moments, including Susan's tenure review, her brother's suicide, my own depression—moments that might have cast an even longer shadow if not for Gabe himself. Attending to his young life brightened every day and helped put those tribulations into perspective. He kept us moving. Moving forward, to be sure, but also backward in the best possible sense, toward treasured yet neglected memories that long predated the attack.

If, for example, I frame my past around the aftermath of that fateful Fourth of July, my father makes just one appearance, on the occasion when I tried, unsuccessfully, to get him to talk to me about supporting a spouse in distress. But as Gabriel's life unfolded, his passion for baseball would send me further into the past, where I rejoined a very different dad. A dad I used to brag about, telling anyone who would listen that he'd pitched two no-hitters in high school and was offered a minor-league contract by the St. Louis Cardinals. He'd played fast-pitch softball into his fifties, thanks to which I once attended a game with my grandfather (his dad), who treated me to a soft-serve vanilla ice-cream cone I can still taste. After work, he'd get no more than halfway from the car to the house before I'd run out and ask if I could pitch to him, knowing he'd say yes despite the chronically bruised shins he owed to this indulgence. Notwithstanding all the cares of adulthood, he became playful as a storyteller, regaling us with tales about baseball at Kodak Park, where George Eastman had allotted land for a stadium on the condition that a fir tree he'd brought back from Japan be left in place—a tree that grew to be gigantic and into whose branches anyone playing right or center field would sooner or later, while chasing a fly ball, disappear altogether.

Gabe never met my father, who would have appreciated how his grandson took to thwacking balls with sticks almost from the moment he could walk. This backyard pursuit prepared him well for T-ball, in which the baseball, instead of being pitched, is simply placed on a post where five- and six-year-olds stand a better chance of hitting it. In the Princeton league, he was drafted by the Expos, named after the Major League Baseball team from Montreal. Gabe's Expos fielded five or six players instead of nine—when they showed up. Even then, it wasn't clear they were all there. The third baseman, for instance, usually sat on the ground in lotus position with his back to home plate, contemplating the clover in left field. At least once, the opposing team in its entirety failed to materialize. Nevertheless the kids got to hit and run and score to their hearts' delight, without getting bogged down in defense. While Gabe and I continued to read at bedtime, my own sense of play found a second home in this love of his, which also created for both of us, in Princeton and Vermont, a community to be part of.

And then, baseball led us in directions wholly unforeseen. A few years after that T-ball draft, Gabe and I drove from Vermont to Montreal to see the major league Expos, thus establishing a connection between baseball and another interest of mine from which it was otherwise worlds removed, namely, the French language. Even when the Expos ceased operations, the French connection remained, sending us farther north to see the Québec Capitales, where I would scarcely remember the game itself for having been so thoroughly absorbed by the French translation of baseball's all-American lingo. Who could fail to be charmed by the word for outfielder, *voltigeur*, which suggests a butterfly or an acrobat? Instead of hot dogs, we had a late, leisurely dinner near the Château Frontenac.

An additional benefit concerned my role as family launderer. Because we were constantly on the move between Vermont and New Jersey, Gabe played in several leagues and for quite a number of teams. Thanks to my efforts, he began every game in a spotless uniform. This should have been satisfaction enough, but was not without its selfish motives. For one thing, doing the laundry was a way for me to maintain my gender-bending fatherhood long after I'd held Gabe in my arms and given him his bottle. For another, since I almost invariably helped coach his teams, I could take pride in my versatility, even see myself reflected in Karl Marx's utopian vision of labor, at once professor, baseball coach, and launderer, all in the same day.

Only once did it appear that my fatherly dedication as a launderer might be put to the test. This was at the start of a fall season in Princeton, when Gabe, long since graduated from T-ball to Little League, came in the door and said, with a sheepish look, "Dad, guess which team I'm on." I knew it wasn't up to him. He'd been drafted again. But he was a native New Englander, which meant there was only one team he could feel sheepish about playing for. A team from New York.

"You're kidding!" I gasped.

"Nope."

I gave him credit. He loved the game more than any team, even the Boston Red Sox. And he would go ahead and play the fall season, as drafted, despite being a citizen of Red Sox Nation.

I gave myself credit, too. He must have known I loved him if he felt safe enough to admit he'd be wearing the garb of a gang his father considered a greater threat to civilization than Darth Vader.

But there was the matter of laundry. Would I send him to the ballpark in a dirty uniform just because it bore the name of a New Englander's anathema? Or would I make sure that my son's Yankees jersey was immaculate every time he stepped on the field?

"So," I said, "where's the shirt? I was just putting a load in the washer."

"But Dad," he exclaimed, "I haven't even worn it yet!"

"Well, let's not take any chances."

I wished my father had been there to enjoy the baseball connection with us. My mother couldn't care less about baseball, having attended far too many of my father's games at Kodak Park, where her scampering sons ended up covered in dust from the crushed cinder around the bleachers and where, she claimed, all of the games went into extra innings. But she took the liveliest pleasure in Gabe, perhaps because she'd grown so skeptical about my ever producing any offspring at all that the intrinsic appeal of this grandchild was enhanced by his unexpectedness. At her house in the Finger Lakes, she reserved a little Adirondack chair for him and made sure the special cupholders were filled with his favorite snacks. She would invite him into her studio and pull out crayons, colored pencils, chalks, and paints so they could make pictures together. Sometimes they'd go outside and wade along the shore, holding hands.

Their relationship touched me all the more as I worried about her, about her solitude, despite the fact that my brother, who lived nearby, dropped in to see her almost every day. She'd been married to our father for forty-nine years, and I couldn't quite imagine what it was like for her to wake up in the morning to a world with so many reminders of his absence. Did she pause and sigh, perched on the edge of their bed, wondering how to go on? Was she forlorn at mealtimes, eating all by herself? With Gabriel she smiled and laughed. The joy she expressed in his presence made me feel as if I was helping take the edge off her loneliness, maybe even repaying in some measure my extraordinary luck in having been raised by such a kind, lovely woman. At the same time I could never watch them together without the peripheral awareness of what her aging told me I was going to lose.

Vulnerability and loss were already in the air when she passed away, in November 2001. Two months before, Susan and I had dropped Gabe off at elementary school in Princeton when the first plane crashed into the North Tower of the World Trade Center. In the afternoon, we picked him up from the school's lockdown, hugging him close. It was never entirely clear how much my mother knew or understood about the terrorist attacks, as she'd been in hospice since August, when she was diagnosed with a very aggressive type of brain cancer. On our short, slow walks outside the hospital, she would take my arm to steady herself and direct my attention to the sky, which, as a painter, she had never tired of looking at. On one occasion she raised her hand to trace the flight of an airplane, then dropped it back to her side, unsure of what she'd seen. I thought maybe it was a hallucination caused by her illness. But it also seemed to me no more unusual to believe in a plane that wasn't there than to look in disbelief, as we had done on 9/11, at a plane that really was.

Many years later, I asked Gabe what, if anything, he remembered about his grandmother's memorial service. He was still a young boy at the time. It turned out he'd been focused on me, wondering what it was like to lose my mother. When I first experienced the death of a grandparent—my paternal grandfather, the jazz pianist, the man who had taken me to watch my dad play baseball and bought me that memorable ice-cream cone—I was already fifteen. Yet I was just as preoccupied with my father as Gabe was with me. Who can say when or how or to what extent the sympathy you feel for your parents at the loss of their own is joined to the visceral awareness that someday you, in turn, will lose *them*. And that, if you yourself become a parent, you'll someday be lost to your children, unable even to comfort them in their grieving. I was certainly prone to such thoughts as family and friends gathered to pay tribute to my mother. The very connectedness affirmed on these occasions attests to people's aloneness.

As Gabe was growing up, Susan and I wondered how and when we'd tell him what happened in the years just before his birth. We'd had plenty of time to think about this, in no hurry to broach the subject before he was old enough to take it in without being too disturbed. The occasion seemed to be in no hurry, either, favoring the procrastinator in both of us, as well as the sense that we'd somehow know what to say when the moment arrived. Whenever I tried to visualize that moment, what I saw was a pretty conventional scene in which the three of us sat down for a heart-to-heart talk.

But nothing of the sort ever took place. The subject did once come up in conversation during the era when, as we cruised along in the car, a question would occasionally be put forward from the back seat about things like infinity or life after death. In this instance, the question may have been prompted by whatever Gabe had learned about the murder of Half and Suzanne Zantop, Dartmouth professors and friends of ours, in their home in January 2001. He asked, "Did anyone ever try to hurt you?" In the driver's seat, I could defer to Susan on the pretext that discussing issues of serious import might distract me from the road and land us all in a ditch. Besides, it made more sense that she answer, since he appeared to be addressing her. "Well," she replied, turning around to face him, "yes, one time in France a man tried to hurt me. But I fought back and got away and afterward I was okay." As her response seemed to satisfy his curiosity, she didn't elaborate.

In retrospect, though, I was struck by how quickly he had then moved on to other things. It seemed that what mattered to him was just knowing his parents were all right, even if bad stuff had happened to them before he was around. And I had no doubt that Susan's response had been calibrated in the full awareness that, for Gabe, she wasn't primarily the woman who'd been hurt but his mother, and that I wasn't the husband who'd seen her hurt but the father of a boy who required, as often as possible, a game of catch in the back yard.

Just because we never had that heart-to-heart talk didn't mean, however, that Gabe learned nothing more about the attack. There were plenty of other sources of information: conversations overheard, alluding either to the event or to Susan's research, which focused on gender-based violence; copies of her book, which could always be found around the house; and, when Gabe was in middle school and high school, the internet. Over time, we suspected he knew more than what little had been divulged in that car ride, but we were never sure how much. We weren't likely to find out, either, once he reached the age at which young people in our culture decide that talking to their parents isn't the first item on their agenda. This adolescent distancing was perfectly normal in a boy who, whatever he'd discovered or failed to discover about his parents, had always struck us as well-adjusted. There was simply no reason to intervene.

Besides, he was mapping out his own itinerary, to the point where it became more a question of what we knew or didn't know about him than the reverse. Often enough, information reached us in unpredictable ways, momentarily illuminating the contours of a whole unsuspected landscape. Thus it would happen, for example, that at some gathering or other the topic of conversation would draw him out and we'd suddenly discover he was remarkably knowledgeable about the science of climate change or the foreign policy of Barack Obama. Although this went some way toward explaining what he devoted so many hours to in his room, it also suggested we might be in the dark about a good deal more. Such as his social life. For despite our spending most of his teen years in a house on the Dartmouth campus, where it was easier to see people of his age than in rural Vermont, he almost never had anybody over. Sometimes we worried: Was he as isolated as this suggested? The extent of our ignorance emerged on parents' night at Hanover High School, when we came across a couple of students whose job it was to guide lost adults like us to the right classroom. They saw our name tags and asked, excitedly, whether we were Gabe's parents. We said yes, expressing surprise that they knew him since we'd sometimes wondered if he had friends. This they found uproariously funny.

At about this time, when talking about the attack was far from my mind, an unforeseen occasion arose. It was one of those lovely summer evenings in Vermont for which you put up with the long winter and the pseudo-spring called mud season. Moments of crystalline light on the meadows and ponds and mountains, when the air is warm, the pace relaxed, and it feels especially good to be alive. The three of us had been invited by friends to dinner at their farm, where we'd enjoyed festive gatherings in the past. They kept cows and chickens and some free-roaming sheep who amused us with their disgruntled bleats.

It was a familiar group of people, a few from our parents' generation, more from ours, several of Gabe's age. Also a husband and wife who were new to me. Before dinner, we were sipping drinks when the conversation turned to France or things French. I believe it started when the woman I'd just met, sitting across from me, asked what I did for a living. At the mere mention of my job, she grew excited, immediately switching into a French that wasn't bad but conveyed a kind of bubbly Francophilia and that, in the midst of people who were less comfortable in the language or didn't know it at all, felt like an invitation to show off. I eased back into English, as gently as I could to avoid being rude, suggesting that I spoke French in professional contexts for the most part. In the hope of changing the subject, I said we didn't spend much time in France anymore, due to an upleasant experience we'd once had there.

It was a mistake to add this last note. I'd wrongly assumed that she would see I was posting a stop sign, when all I did in fact was fuel her curiosity. She insisted, inquiring earnestly from the edge of her seat while others listened, "Oh, what happened?" "Actually, I'd rather not go into it," I replied. Not to be deterred, she enthused, "Aw, c'mon, tell us!" It was all I could do just to mutter, "I really don't want to talk about it." Still she didn't back off.

Hadn't I made myself clear? Couldn't she see I wasn't in the mood to share this with a complete stranger, much less in the midst of a happy summertime get-together? Did she think I'd be so reticent about some minor mishap? Did she imagine that, because it had taken place in France, the experience in question could be spoken of in the same breath as baguettes, Brie, and Beaujolais?

In my jaw, at my temples, around my forehead, I felt a constriction reminiscent of other moments over the years when I'd encountered insensitive responses to Susan's story. And in this instance the story hadn't even been told yet! What set me off was the invasion of privacy. I was suddenly speechless with anger at this woman who had intruded into a deeply personal matter I hadn't even discussed with my own son, not to mention all the other people in the room.

The awkward silence was broken by Susan, seated off to my right. "I was the victim of a sexual assault and attempted murder."

I don't recall the reaction. I was looking at the floor, trying to tune it all out, wishing there was an easy, inconspicuous way to exit the room. Then I noticed the woman swivel toward Gabe, sitting next to me on the left, and heard her ask him, "How did this affect you growing up?"

"Well," he answered, "I knew the gist of what happened. But it always seemed to me that they were doing fine, so I didn't worry."

My eyes hadn't left the floor, and probably spent most of their time there until we were called to dinner. I remember little else from the evening besides this initial scene, no doubt because my mind stayed busy taking it all in, including what Gabe had said. The point I kept coming back to was that, in the space of a few seconds, he had relieved concerns I hadn't realized were still weighing on me after so many years. Who knows? It may even be that my anger at the woman was due not only to her intrusion into our private life but to her having unwittingly drawn my attention to what I considered a failure of mine as a parent. Maybe I was mad at myself for not having spoken with Gabe long before this stranger brought the story up in public and in such an untimely way. Be that as it may, Gabe's words were like a balm. It was as if he'd turned to face me and declared, "Look! I'm fine! See? You can stop worrying."

I know now that things were not so simple. Based on the little we'd given him to go on, he'd had to develop his own understanding of what had happened in France and how we'd coped with it, all the while sensing, perhaps from our own reticence, that talking could be fraught. Even the moment I've just described was a difficult one for him, since the poise with which he spoke required overcoming the agitation he'd picked up from me. As we left the house, he strode up beside me and exclaimed, "Boy, you were really angry!" I mumbled some sort of excuse: the woman was overbearing, or the occasion wasn't suitable, I don't recall. All I felt right then was gratitude to him.

By then Gabe was in his junior or senior year of high school. I ought to know which one it was. Realizing I couldn't determine this on my own reminds me of parents who, at major milestones in their children's lives, wonder where the time has gone, how it could be such a blur. A commonplace, a cliché, to be sure—but maybe also, more charitably viewed, just a place held in common with those who share a certain sense of the years slipping by.

In any case the whole process of researching and visiting and applying to colleges was either in the offing or already underway. Susan and I were generally kept at arm's length throughout. I suppose that just having professors as parents would be enough to make you want to plot your own course. One thing was clear: Gabe didn't have his eye on Dartmouth or Princeton. But we didn't even find out he'd decided on Kenyon until two or three weeks after he'd received the offer of admission with a merit scholarship.

As his departure loomed, it helped to be distracted by practicalities: making sure to buy twin XL sheets, remembering to pack the laptop, finding a place in the car for the last box of books. It also helped to look forward to his first holiday return, and to glance around and see how much of him was staying with us, including thousands of baseball cards.

Since Susan had to fly to Denver to help her parents settle into assisted living, Gabe and I made the long trip from northern New England to central Ohio by ourselves. Baseball provided a pretext for breaking it up. The idea was Gabe's, and felt like a thoughtful way to reassure me that what we'd always shared was still there and always would be. We'd visited Cooperstown on quite a few occasions, but this time we drove down to Connecticut to watch the Bridgeport Bluefish, stayed overnight in Pennsylvania, then made our way the next morning to the Little League World Series in Williamsport. Gabe bought me a stylish shirt like the blue one worn by the team from Curaçao (a shirt that's always been as clean as his uniforms, but for a different reason, which is that I almost never wear it for fear of the color fading in the wash). In the evening we attended a professional game in eastern Ohio between the Mahoning Valley Scrappers and the Jamestown Jammers, where I was reminded of how much, thanks to Gabe, I'd come to appreciate the ease and friendliness of minor-league venues. As we pulled into the parking lot, the attendant, having caught sight of our license plates, let us know how impressed and gratified she was that we had driven all the way from Vermont just to watch their boys play. The occasion gave me the chance as well to further my education in minor-league team names, adding to a list that already included not only our own Vermont Lake Monsters but also such standouts as the Lansing Lugnuts and the Batavia Muckdogs. I hadn't actually reflected on *Jammers*. It seemed somehow to lack the aggressive spirit found in the names of so many sports teams. And although, from talking to my brother, who worked in the wine industry, I was vaguely aware of agriculture in the area of Jamestown, New York, I couldn't at all make out the logo on the Jammers' caps. "Oh," Gabe explained, "it's a bunch of grapes," adding, "a really *angry* bunch of grapes."

We arrived on the Kenyon campus the next morning so he could participate in a pre-orientation program. Susan was scheduled to come into town that evening. I took the opportunity of a free afternoon to go for a long run, so long that I had to walk the last uphill stretch to the inn on campus. As I hiked up the left shoulder, I noticed a group of fifteen or twenty spirited students coming down the opposite side of the road. Among them I suddenly picked out Gabe. I could have sworn he saw me, too—that our gazes met for a split second, before he looked away and melded back into the group. Smiling to myself, I imagined him thinking, Will I never be free of these people? I could understand his impatience. I'd been in his shoes. I knew what an embarrassment parents could be. But whether I'd imagined correctly or not, the fact remained that I was now the parent, that the shoes were his, not mine, and that, whereas he was ready for this, I was reluctant. I simply had to resign myself to parting with our only child, who had brought us the happiness we had once despaired of ever feeling again. Yes, I lectured myself, he has to go away if he's ever going to come back. He has to go away if you're going to see him again. But will he come back? Will I see him? Enough, I lectured again. No lachrymose laments. Yet this didn't make it any easier to acknowledge that I'd just caught my last glimpse of the Gabe we knew.

The next day, we met him on the terrace outside Gund Commons. As I recall, this had been designated as a meeting place where parents scrambling to hold on could say goodbye to children yearning to cut loose. Gabe was distant. He didn't make much eye contact, had little to say. I felt bad for Susan, who had been unable to make the road trip with us and must have found the separation more abrupt. But even if Gabe had been at his most solicitous and affectionate, we would still have returned to our bed-and-breakfast in a state of unmitigated emotional wreckage. We would still have held each other and cried for an hour.

13 *Untimeliness*

Spectators would line both sides of the road, most of them standing, some sitting in lawn chairs, all with an unobstructed view of the parade. It was a modest, small-town Independence Day parade, but no one liked it any the less for that. In addition to marching groups, there were vintage automobiles polished to perfection, floats towed by pickup trucks, fire engines, horses, cows, and a profusion of American flags. For kids, the highlight was the candy of all sorts that would now and then come sailing through the air. Thrown from the cars or floats, it sent them scrambling left and right in the hope of a harvest second only to Halloween. When at last all of the parade entrants had filed by, people would make their way to the town common for a chicken barbecue.

We took Gabriel to this Fourth of July parade, held in a neighboring Vermont village, for as many years as he found the candy irresistible. With him, I could appreciate the ritual, even though it fell on the anniversary of Susan's attack, a day when fun was otherwise foreign to my frame of mind. And oddly enough, making allowance for the festive mood of the parade didn't narrow the gulf between that mood and the reflectiveness with which Susan and I privately marked the occasion. It just led me to wonder how the human organism could inhabit simultaneously two such antithetical realms, or why anniversaries, based as they are on a collective calendar, play so important a role in the commemoration of deeply individualized trauma.

Some July 4ths were sunny and warm, like the day of the attack. On days like that, sensory impressions and the memories associated with them could return from long ago. But any given July 4th could just as well be rainy, and the warm, sunny day reminiscent of the attack could just as well show up in the middle of August. So it was another kind of sameness that mattered. July 4th had to be July 4th regardless of the weather or anything that came with it. It was a placeholder, a date fixed unswervingly in the yearly orbit that returned us to ourselves, to each other. Maybe this was why all of the anniversaries blended into a single image for me: Susan and I sitting outside, with a view of the New England landscape, holding hands, sounding out each other's feelings, taking a moment to think about the loss that was now a part of us. A part of us, but not all of us, for the anniversary was also an occasion to frame, retrospectively, the chaos of that particular July 4th, a chance to enclose within a calendar the remembered irrelevance of all calendars.

Yet the sameness of the date must have served, too, as a yardstick to measure difference from one year to the next. Otherwise, why would people bother to distinguish between numbered anniversaries? Merely for a sense of accomplishment? There's no question that whenever Susan and I sat down on July 4th to think about the disaster, the memories we retrieved had evolved because we ourselves had changed. And it seems safe to say that as a general rule, these memories gradually diminished in number and intensity. On one occasion, quite a few years after the attack, Susan even forgot it was July 4th. This, to my mind, was a sign of recovery.

We'd learned, of course, to be wary of expectations, in regard to recovery as to other matters. The first six months after the assault not only failed to bring about the convalescence we'd envisioned but marked a serious deterioration for both of us. And in the years thereafter the leaden woe of that period revisited us more than once, unannounced. Yet the undermining of expectations could work the other way, too: we may have anticipated feeling pretty upset on the first anniversary of the assault, whereas it turned out not to be a bad day after all. Perhaps because it was unforeseen to begin with, the event tended to return in its own, untimely way. The aftermath just couldn't be scheduled.

I don't mean to say that the "return" of trauma, whatever form it may take, defies all prediction. It's certainly possible to foresee how some situations may revive sensory or affective or other mental traces of the event. But these very traces may also preempt foresight, dispossessing the mind of its ability to distinguish present from past. In my case—and with the major exception of Susan's tenure review—the situations tended to be of a banal, everyday sort, for which the prototype had been firmly established, namely: Susan is late. So it was that one evening, a little more than a year after the attack, as we'd been walking around Woodstock, Vermont, and were drawn momentarily in different directions, we made a plan to meet at a restaurant at 6 o'clock, which is when I showed up, alone. By the time she arrived—at 6:03—I was mad, my heart racing. I immediately complained about the delay. It was less a matter of the three minutes than of her overlooking my vulnerability to the mere suggestion of her disappearance. I was practically hysterical. Needless to say this did not sit well with her. Who could live with such a person? And how had I let myself be turned into such a caricature of the controlling male? In three minutes!

Outbursts like this were so incongruous or disproportionate in character, and the price I paid for them so steep in remorse and shame, that I simply had to find a way to account for them, if only in the hope of reducing their frequency and severity. I had to ask myself if there might have been something from *before* Susan's attack that was compounding its effects on me. Later, when I began to study the clinical literature on trauma, I discovered in the notion of premorbidity what should already have been obvious—that the response to a traumatic event (the post-traumatic pathology or "morbidity") depends to an important degree on the patient's history. So although I wouldn't yet have stated it this way, I was essentially seeking an answer to the question, Who was I before I became morbid?

On that fateful day, after feeling a slight annoyance at Susan for taking a walk I thought ill-timed, I passed through stages: first, puzzlement at why she hadn't returned when expected; next, a worry growing slowly but inexorably into full-fledged anxiety; and finally, a tipping, a cascading in the direction of barely contained panic. Those who have found themselves in a similar situation—involving a loved one suddenly unaccounted for—may recognize the sequence. I crossed from one end to the other very fast, due in part, I think, to the unfamiliarity of our surroundings, but also to a particular susceptibility I only learned to appreciate when I saw a psychiatrist, Dr. Max Day, around the time of the Woodstock incident.

At our first meeting, Dr. Day began by gathering some basic information, then caught me off guard: "Did you ever wet your bed?"

I'd never been asked that question, in or out of therapy. Well, no, I replied, I wasn't a bedwetter. Then I corrected myself, telling Dr. Day it had happened just once, during summer camp when I was eight or nine years old. Every night for a week, in my sleeping bag. It was disgusting. As soon as I woke up I stole out of the cabin and draped the sleeping bag over a clothesline to let it dry and air out. But there was no way to wash it, and sometimes, to my embarrassment, a cabinmate would get a whiff and rib me about it.

Dr. Day continued: "Do you recall anything else from camp that summer? Anything that really stood out? Something that might have upset you?"

That's when I remembered the sleep-out, which I'd never connected to the bedwetting. "We were halfway up this mountain," I began. "It was late and the campfire had died down. Just before sending us off to our sleeping bags, the cabin counselor urged us to think about this: 'Where will you be if Jesus comes back tonight?'"

"The ground was hard. It was pitch dark and chilly. The campers were all quiet around me but I kept hearing mysterious noises in the woods. Plus, I knew there were bears. And now this: 'Where will you be if Jesus comes back tonight?'"

Dr. Day interrupted: "But why was this so upsetting? Wasn't it a good thing if Jesus came back?"

"That depended! If you were saved, then it was a good thing because you got to go to heaven. If you weren't saved, it was bad news because you were stuck on earth when all hell was supposed to break loose—first the Tribulation, then Armageddon. Besides, the Rapture takes places in 'the twinkling of an eye,' a nanosecond. Nobody knows when it's coming, and if you're left behind you only find out it's occurred when you happen to notice that certain people—the lucky few—have disappeared from the face of the earth.

For me, on the mountain, this would have meant being abandoned forever by my parents. And the fact is I don't even remember if I was saved or not, which just goes to show that, either way, the Rapture scared the piss out of me—no pun intended. I hardly slept a wink that night."

Dr. Day nodded. "So there was just the one time you wet your bed. Was it also the only time you were scared like this?"

"No, not at all. The worst was earlier. I couldn't have been more than five or six. Even so, I already knew about the Rapture, since people in our church never stopped talking about it."

The incident, I told Dr. Day, had to do with a neighbor who, once every summer, took a group of kids for an afternoon outing at the local amusement park. On this occasion I ran home to ask my parents if it was okay for me to go. But they were nowhere to be found. Not in the house, not in the garage, the backyard, the front yard. Both of my brothers had disappeared, too. We were the only born-again Christians I knew on the whole block. Everybody else, including the neighbor, was Catholic. We were on perfectly good terms with them, but somehow I'd gathered they weren't like us. So the fact that they were still around didn't reassure me.

"I think it was when I couldn't find even one of my brothers that I lost it. This was the end. I'd been left behind. You know, the night on the mountain was very frightening. This was terrifying."

Eventually, distraught and sobbing, I located my parents. In their bedroom—sitting in the *bed* in their bedroom, under a sheet, in the middle of the afternoon, which was really weird. For some reason they seemed to be very happy. I let them know I wasn't.

But by now there was just enough left of the session with Dr. Day for me to explain what I'd come for in the first place and hoped to talk about the next time. When I told him what had happened to

Susan, he was shocked, despite his many years of listening to awful stories. He just stared at me and sighed, "It's a vale of tears."

For purely practical reasons, I never saw Dr. Day again. He was in Newton, Massachusetts, and I was either in northern New England or southern New Jersey. But I'd been reminded of how my fundamentalist upbringing had magnified in me every child's worst fear. And of how, on leaving the church at the age of fifteen, I had assumed I was leaving the fear as well, doubtless still too young to ask myself whether a system of belief drilled into a child might produce a neurological imprint that could never be excised. As I had learned since then, the anxiety of apocalypse I'd acquired from Biblical prophecy no longer needed prophecy to be aroused. It could roam at will, in search of a suitable pretext. Standing out on that road in St.-Geoirs, with the minutes ticking by, I was the easiest prey in the world.

Almost thirty years after the restaurant scene in Woodstock (although by no means for the first time since then), I fell into the trap again, aggrieved when Susan returned from a trip to Western Massachusetts an hour or more later than I'd been led to expect. As ominous for me as the old familiar fear or anger itself was the sense that I could do nothing to arrest its upswelling, as if I were the mere host of a pathogen especially adept at quickening my pulse, elevating my irritability, confounding my judgment, distracting me from everything except what I least wanted to focus on—an invader that, once battle was joined, would surely win. It was just a matter of time before the clock stopped, before I found myself back in another kind of time, one that seemed never to pass and in which, by definition, it was always too late. On arrival, Susan wisely read the situation and, in short order, restored me to reality. But I was taken aback all the same to witness this regression of mine, to see how a single moment could expand its boundaries to the horizon while making a thirty-year interval look infinitesimal.

This was not a common occurrence, fortunately. What made it worrisome was the speed and tenacity with which, as if by an autonomic response, I had reverted to an apocalyptic story line when faced with the unexpected. If this reaction can be said to have served a purpose, it was in reminding me that the attack—the most unforeseen, unpredictable, unscripted event of my whole adult life—could become a scenario in its own right. And that recovery entailed the disarming of that scenario. Somehow I had to learn, against my own resistance at once psychological and somatic, that life after the event was as unscripted as the event itself. I'm still working on it.

Emotional flashbacks are a common symptom of PTSD. So are dreams that represent the event in realistic or at least recognizable form. I never had a single dream even remotely related to the attack, however. Nor did Susan, with one exception. This may be attributable to benzodiazepines, which we were first prescribed in the hospital, and which make me think that my "Ode to Lexomil" wasn't such a bad idea. In Susan's dream, which may even have been gratifying to some extent, she used her recently acquired self-defense techniques against the attacker.

But I did once have a waking nightmare, which, unlike a lifelike dream, was so enigmatically encoded that I've never fully disentangled the threads connecting it to the attack—and perhaps for good reason, since the impenetrability itself, the not knowing what was going on, lay at the core of my helplessness, and could therefore have been among those threads.

This happened during the year when Susan's assailant was tried and I came up for tenure. On an overcast and chilly day in Princeton,

I took our Dalmatians for a regular afternoon outing near the towpath between Lake Carnegie and the Delaware and Raritan Canal. I was wearing my ski jacket over a sweater, the collar turned up. I parked in the small lot next to the canal, then steered the dogs away from the towpath in case an unsuspecting stranger materialized. We headed up onto a big open area, where they'd have plenty of room to roam and where I was counting on the chain-link fence around the athletic fields to prevent them from jumping on Ultimate Frisbee players. But I didn't see anybody there. My mind at ease, I unleashed the hounds.

They bolted like horses from a starting gate. Each on his own, they scampered every which way, at the mercy of a short attention span and a hypersensitive olfactory cortex. I ambled along, my hands clasped behind my back, holding the leashes. Rather than try to keep up, I remained between them and the towpath as well as the road, where only calamity could await.

As I looked around, the landscape struck me as insufferably drab, which it tends to be for much of the year in the northeast. The only color worthy of the name was the turquoise of my parka. I was shaking my head, wondering how I'd managed to spend most of my life in such a deflating ecosystem, when I picked up, then shrugged off, some yelping. At times, the dogs yelped.

Yet a yelp is a short-lived thing, whereas the chorus I heard kept going. I walked toward the dogs, some thirty yards away, curious to discover what had prompted the outcry. They kept lunging and backpedaling, as if they couldn't decide whether to attack or retreat. I was puzzled, unable to see anything, but increasingly alarmed by their frenzy. I was practically upon them when I detected a ripple in the grass, then a moving shape. A groundhog. Bloodied and desperate.

Heart suddenly pounding, I jumped in. But the odds were against me and against the poor animal. No sooner did I corner one of the dogs, trying to clip a leash to its collar, than the other went back at the groundhog, which was trying to defend itself while inching backward toward its hole. Distracted by this face-off, I lost my grip on the dog I had, and the round began again. If I didn't stop it the groundhog was going to die. Desperate and enraged, I screamed, "Max! Dexter!" They had blood on their muzzles. Blood was flying through the air, some of it landing on me.

Finally, I tackled Max and held on, winding the leash around my wrist. He sat next to me, panting, while I kneeled, my forehead almost touching the ground. I was heaving, gasping for air, expecting at any moment to black out or have one of those heart attacks that had killed my father and my grandfather. All of this for a groundhog. Yet I hoped it had somehow escaped Dexter's clutches, wherever Dexter was.

Then a voice. A woman's voice. And here I'd thought I was alone. Still on my knees, I tilted my head up, trying to focus through the sweat dripping into my eyes. She was young, maybe in her late twenties. Otherwise, I remember nothing but her solicitousness. She was leading Dexter toward me, having somehow got hold of the leash I'd clipped on him only to have it ripped out of my hand. She said, "I'm sorry, sir." Sorry? What was she sorry about? Where had she come from? Who was she?

Everything had happened so fast that the data continued to clog my cerebral intake, waiting to be processed. I seemed to have glimpsed, in the chaos, a cluster of people far away, on the other side of the playing fields. Since the fields were cambered, higher in the middle than at the edges, I had only a sketchy view of them. But now another moment came to mind, when I was peripherally aware that these people were running toward me, yelling. One of them split off from the group. It must have been this woman. A teacher? A chaperone? She must have come through a gate to help me.

I stood up, took Dexter's leash, thanked her. I was still short of breath, sweating profusely, and could feel tears welling up.

By now the group, a bunch of teenagers, had reached the nearest fence, only ten yards from where I was standing. It was a high fence, and a boy, seventeen or eighteen, had taken hold of it, his fingers curled around the steel links. He was full-grown, lanky, with hair almost shoulder-length, just like mine when I went off to college. He was shaking the fence as if trying to wrench it right out of the ground. And he was screaming at me.

I don't recall the exact words, but the message was clear: I was an asshole. I beat my dogs. I yelled at them and kicked at them and cuffed them. I was an animal abuser. An asshole.

The anger aroused in me by the attack had more or less subsided due to sheer exhaustion. But now it redoubled at this false accusation. To be vilified for cruelty to animals when I'd just been trying to save one of them was more than enough to set me off. Walking the dogs back to the car, I looked at the kid and shouted, "If you're so worried about cruelty to animals then why the hell didn't you come help me instead of yelling your head off?! Fuck you!"

I was just turning my back on a crescendo of recriminations when I heard the woman's voice again. "I'm really sorry, sir."

When did it sink in? As I was driving home with the dogs? Relating the adventure to Susan? Even later? Why did the woman say "I'm sorry" *after* my confrontation with the kid? As if she was sorry for something besides the episode with the dogs and the groundhog. As if she was apologizing for the kid. And for the others. Maybe even for herself. Because they had all misunderstood.

From where they were standing, and then running, there *was* no groundhog. All they could see was a man lashing out at a couple of Dalmatians. By coming through the gate, she alone had been able to spot the poor rodent, for just long enough to realize that this drama didn't have to do with a man who abused animals.

I didn't envy her. She clearly played some supervisory role with this group. And now she had one hell of a teaching moment on her hands. What did she do next? Sit them down in a circle to discuss what happened? To explain the misunderstanding? To weigh the moral ambiguities?

Yet I've always been mesmerized by her voice. Her simple words: "I'm sorry." The first time I heard this it was devoid of any context. What was she sorry for? The second time, I still wasn't sure. And the sense I later attributed to her words never canceled this initial delay in understanding, which became a permanent feature of my memory and made the statement itself strangely abstract and hence transferable to other places where I'd needed so badly to hear it. "I'm sorry, sir. I'm sorry your wife was raped and beaten. I'm sorry for the distress this has caused you. I'm sorry people don't see it. I'm really sorry."

At the same time I've been haunted by the kid, the spitting image of my college-aged self. It's true he misjudged me and cursed me. But the first thing wasn't his fault and the second he did because he had a heart and a conscience. He didn't deserve what he got from me. Yet there was nothing to be done. From the moment I jumped into the fray, determined to collar the dogs, there sprang from within me an increasingly maddened doppelgänger whose existence could never have been explained to the woman or her youngsters or anybody else because it was born of a furious helplessness that predated this fracas. And the redoubling of my anger didn't just have to do with being accused of a specific act that day but of feeling charged, since long before, with complicity in a whole world of violence. I would never have retained so clearly the uncanny resemblance between my accuser and me if it hadn't conjured my own remorseful self-perception in the aftermath of Susan's attack. But of course I couldn't expect people to understand that. I couldn't very well have said to the kid that I'd lost it with my dogs because my wife had been raped in France. For anyone except me, and possibly Susan, this event and my personal backstory were mutually untranslatable.

The moment has stayed with me, perhaps because no effort to grasp it can circumvent my memory of the rage itself or of the terrible sadness that followed. In one of Olga Tokarczuk's novels, the narrator reflects that "anger always leaves a large void behind it, into which a flood of sorrow pours instantly, and keeps on flowing like a great river, without beginning or end."[1]

Whatever *untimely* is taken to mean—unseasonable, inopportune, incongruous, inappropriate—it usually refers to something of a punctual nature: an event, a development, a behavior, an action, something that momentarily interrupts or disrupts the normal course of things. Thinking about post-traumatic time exclusively in terms of discrete moments can be habit-forming, however, depriving that time of its very untimeliness. We imagine we're on firm conceptual ground when perhaps what's out of joint is not just a moment but the course of things in its entirety.

When we returned to Princeton after my unproductive two-year leave, I was nearing the point on the career calendar where an associate professor is expected to give some evidence of promotability to full professor. At the rate I was going, though, I'd still be staffing the middle ranks when the Office of Human Resources mailed me time-sensitive material about retirement. I'd heard stories of men who parried personal or familial turmoil by throwing themselves into their work. With the sense I had of the fragility and brevity of life, I couldn't do it. I wasn't willing to sacrifice the pleasure of my hours with Susan and Gabriel, and I'd also come to regard career matters from a rather jaded point of view. Scholarship as I knew it seemed pointless, like the vanity decried in the Book of Ecclesiastes. And to pursue it when the world was such a colossal mess would tarnish it with another vanity, the egotistical kind.

Granted, I may have perceived as personal vanity what was really no more than the confidence and the commitment required for serious work. My failure to accomplish much at all had left me with such diminished self-respect that I might easily have mistaken a normal ego for an inflated one. The only certainty to which I could cling was that my interest in scholarship stood little chance of resuscitation unless I turned to something of tangible consequence outside the gates of the academy. A few years before, with my customary work at an impasse, I'd discovered Charlotte Delbo's trilogy of memoirs, *Auschwitz and After*, and become so engrossed as to envision a new and very different kind of project. But my excitement had then been dampened by the awareness that trauma studies was already a big field, and Holocaust studies a huge one. What could I possibly contribute? It would take forever to retool, to understand the issues, to find something to say. Simply having the urge to press forward didn't make the prospect of doing so look any less like walking up the down escalator.

But I persisted, and for a very long time. I must have hoped, naively, that making trauma the object of my scholarly research would eventually alleviate the distress of living it. Even so, this hardly explained the particular path I chose. Why study the Holocaust when a great number and variety of other traumatic events were worthy of attention? There were certainly practical reasons: my research had always focused on Europe, which is where the Holocaust took place; I happened to be a specialist of the twentieth century, which is when it took place; and France, the country I knew best, had played a major role in the event. If I was going to invest years of my life in a book related to trauma, I'd better start with some intellectual capital. Yet what lay behind this common sense was a salvage operation. The capital I had in mind amounted to remnants of a former self, a self that had become increasingly illegible except between the lines of our story. To select a project that would draw on training begun as far back as my college days was to stake a claim, in the long shadow of Susan's attack, to something I could call my own.

That I had so personal or existential a stake in this work didn't mean I was always aware of it. But it was brought home to me one day when Susan mentioned a conversation she'd just had about the attack and its aftermath with a female colleague. Informed that I was working on the Holocaust, the woman had remarked, "That's weird!" To understand exactly what she meant would require reconstructing the conversation, which is impossible. At the time, though, I could have asked Susan what she thought the woman had in mind. Was it weird because my previous work had little if anything to do with trauma? Was it weird because she thought of trauma as Susan's domain, on which I was impinging? I could also have asked myself whether it mattered that a woman had said this rather than a man. Yet without the slightest pause I'd taken the remark to imply that it was unsuitable or even perverse for me to be concerned with anything except sexual violence against women. It felt as if I'd just encountered a new mode of invisibility. I fulminated. "What is that supposed to mean? Who is she to judge what I should be doing or not doing? Did it even occur to her that I might have interests of my own?"

With the Holocaust project, I'd begun to find a voice by changing the subject. I'd already spent countless hours listening to Susan and her many other listeners: medical personnel, police officers, lawyers, crisis counselors, couples therapists, family members, friends, acquaintances, colleagues, a judge and jury. But it was easier to express what I'd learned as a listener by turning to survivors whose experience and testimony were far removed from both of us, all the more as Susan already spoke with such authority about violence against women. It was no small thing for me to be able to talk about trauma. I didn't appreciate being told—for whatever reason—that working on the Holocaust was weird.

In the end I did write a book about listening to Holocaust survivors—a subject to which I'll return in the next chapter. But between the publication of that book and the one on Beckett, which appeared just months after Susan's attack, so many years had elapsed that I actually had to do the math. Measured against normal expectations, the interval was outlandishly lengthy. No matter how deeply committed I was to this second book, and no matter how well it was received, I would never make it back to the career that had been scripted for me as far back as graduate school. I'd never make it back to where I thought I should be. Never. I found it embarrassing, even shameful.

The whole thing came into its sharpest focus when I sat down to write a self-evaluation for promotion to full professor. This was really a kind of career narrative, designed to give the candidate a voice in the process, a chance to answer the question: What have you accomplished since tenure? What do you have to show for yourself?

It seemed as if the only way to account for my extraordinary delay in reaching this point would be to tell a story that was institutionally irrelevant. What had I accomplished? What did I have to show for myself? I'll tell you what: I survived the sexual assault and attempted murder of my beloved spouse, that's what. But no, that wasn't quite right. What I really wanted to say was: My spouse and I, together, rebuilt our lives after she was raped and almost killed.

This would never do, of course. Even though the strict distinction between the personal and the professional had ceased long ago to make sense to me, I had to respect the nature of the exercise, and alluded just once, in drafting my self-evaluation, to "unforeseen events" that had motivated a change in intellectual orientation, otherwise leaving it to my superiors to make what they would of my being so far off schedule.

But as I drew this self-portrait, something shifted. I asked myself: Are these black-robed judges—the ones looking down at me and scowling—are they really there? Or are they entirely of my own invention? To whom do I feel the need to apologize, to offer excuses? And why, after all these years, am I still such a sucker for the success stories that make my own story look like an aberration? The indignation aroused by these questions, strong enough that I'd have to leave my desk and go for a brisk walk or even a strenuous run, suggested that perhaps there was no reason to believe it should have gone otherwise, no reason to think I must still somehow fix what was simply my life—not a detour or an aberration but, for me, the very course of things, the way they'd ended up, the untimely hand I'd been dealt. My life. Occasionally, after walking or running, I'd even feel at peace, as if forgiven. It was a sensation that would take some getting used to.

14 *Second Thoughts*

In the preface to *Aftermath*, Susan notes, in reference to the ten-year period over which she was writing the book: "I have changed during this time and so have my views, but, rather than revise my earlier writings in light of more recent understandings, I have tried to convey the trajectory of my ideas." Further on, describing chapter 1, drafted during the first two years following the assault, she says: "This chapter would be different in many ways were I to write it now—less angry, less urgent, and somewhat more detached. But I have left it in its original form . . . in order to convey my perspective soon after the event."[1] For this she was roundly criticized by a reviewer, who felt that she should *not* have left that chapter in its original form, that she should indeed have revised her earlier writings in light of more recent understandings. It seemed to have escaped the reviewer that, in a work as much narrative as philosophical, the destination was indissociable from the itinerary that led to it. No doubt the assumption was that Susan's current views had rendered her previous ones somehow deficient or untrustworthy (all the more so if they had been informed by anger or urgency). On this premise, one could go so far as to say that Susan should not have published the book at all, since presumably her views would continue to evolve, with the result that not just a chapter or two but the entirety of *Aftermath* would someday be rendered suspect.

I have always appreciated the wisdom of Susan's decision to honor a time-bound truth (at the risk—very real, as it turned out—of being misunderstood). What has stayed with me above all is the notion of trajectory, of the survivor's ongoing reinterpretation of her experience. I picture it as a kind of epistemic nesting, whereby the most recent understanding of a state of affairs reframes—without falsifying—its predecessors, and is eventually reframed in its turn. Writing at a distance of thirty years after the attack, I've had plenty of time to ponder my own trajectory, to consider how changes of perspective have affected my life even as they became a part of it. These changes have been like second thoughts, shifts of position that call previous views into question without claiming the last word for themselves. They've taught me things about trauma that I couldn't have learned in any other way.

In late October 2007, I received an invitation to speak at a colloquium in honor of Philippe, who had died in January. It came, coincidentally, in an email from the very person who had visited Philippe and Claire right after we left St.-Geoirs, the person about whom Claire had written that they "kept her on a leash," never letting her stray from the house "without a bodyguard." The event would take place in April 2008, in New York. I replied in December, saying I wasn't sure I could attend but would know after New Year's. In February, I declined the invitation, explaining that my family schedule made it impossible for me to be there.

This was stretching it. True, I was commuting between Princeton and Hanover every week and was reluctant to sacrifice time with Susan and Gabriel. Yet they would surely have forgiven me if I'd skipped a visit or just curtailed it. The fact was that it took me three months to utter a simple *yes* or *no*, and even then I was unable to state the real reason. This was sufficient proof that the October invitation had provoked a crisis of sorts.

On the face of it, the colloquium offered a fine opportunity to pay tribute to Philippe, to demonstrate my friendship for him, to preserve our ties despite his absence. Still, I knew when I received the invitation that I couldn't possibly accept it and that I'd have to say goodbye again as I had done when he died, by myself and in silence. It wasn't that we'd had a falling out, as Susan and I had suffered with Claire. He and I had continued to correspond, at more or less extended intervals. Yet the balance of the relationship had shifted away from shared intellectual interests toward personal matters, especially the attack and its aftermath, which I wasn't about to air on such an occasion—or to suppress, either. And it didn't help that Claire would be attending. The chasm that had opened between us was so wide that I could no more imagine speaking to her than to an audience of scholars, and even worried that trying to bridge it could rub Susan the wrong way. I had to face it: the door to this venue was closed.

Far from clarifying matters, though, the crisis revived an emotional confusion as fresh as when it had first been aroused long ago, as if in all that time I hadn't sorted any of it out. And now, instead of making an effort to do so, I just held my breath until the colloquium was a thing of the past, then went on with my life.

One evening twelve years later, in 2020, Susan and I were talking when the discussion suddenly turned—I don't recall how or why—to Philippe and Claire. I was distracted by dinner preparations so she had to stop me between the stove and the refrigerator to make sure I registered what she'd just said. "I mean it. I'm sorry."

Sorry for what had happened to my friendship with them, for the position I'd been put in to begin with. Always the mediator, exposed to the displeasure of both parties. Trying, in contentious exchanges with Susan, to allow for cultural miscommunication, to emphasize Claire and Philippe's affection and devotion, to recall the extraordinary lengths to which Claire had gone to support us during those eleven days—but to no avail, since everything was overshadowed, for both of us, by Claire's visit with the assailant's parents and her poorly chosen phrase "my distant cousins." Yes, I remembered the loneliness of the go-between. And I regretted that our friendship had turned out to be a casualty of the attack.

But I wasn't at all upset with Susan. Just the opposite: I was touched by her sympathy and by her willingness to imagine what it had been like for me. And somehow this freed me from the muddled perspective to which I'd been confined by mediation. No longer in the middle, I could look at what had happened with a new set of eyes and try to understand how people who cared for each other and shared a good deal in their ethical and political views had become permanently estranged by a traumatic event.

I reread Claire's letters. Referring in one of them to the assailant's parents, she spoke of "a crushing sense of shame" and of "stunned incomprehension." She observed that their lives were "ruined forever by the horrific act their son had committed." There was even a parenthetical note saying that, in their concern for the victim, they had asked for news of "la dame." All of this was coupled with Claire's insistence that she would have listened to anyone who had come to her in their condition because she saw in them—in their abject poverty, their isolation, the violence and alcoholism in their family, their cluelessness about medical and other resources—victims of a social injustice for which she felt responsible. Of course, this was the same letter I'd read just six months after the attack, when I didn't want to hear a word about these people. Back then, to speak in the same breath of their plight and Susan's was, for me, to blur the very category of victim, to relativize Susan's suffering, even to suggest that there were two equivalent sides to the story. It left me indignant, to say the least. But although, these many years later, I recalled perfectly well my feelings at the moment, I no longer *felt* them. Which didn't mean I could now put the whole matter behind me. It was just that, with those feelings somehow cleared away by the passage of time, I could see there was still something amiss, even if I didn't know quite what it was. I decided to take another look at some letters I'd later received from Philippe.

Three years after the attack, he wrote to thank me for the English translation of his book, the one we'd been working on when Susan went out for a walk, which had now appeared in print. He mentioned, in the same letter, having seen a press release about the trial, of which we'd said nothing since the falling out with Claire. Both of them, he noted, were "scandalisés" by the lightness of the sentence (ten years). More than a year later, after a delay due to health problems, he wrote me again. This time he was responding to a letter I'd sent in reply to his previous one, in which I'd asked him a question he now quoted verbatim: "How can you be scandalized by the outcome of the trial after having granted so much importance to 'extenuating circumstances'?" The question was unfair, in a way, because I used the plural *vous*, thus tacitly assuming complete agreement between him and Claire—but also because neither of them had ever alluded to extenuating circumstances in the strict, juridical sense of the term. "And for good reason," Philippe wrote, "since there are no such circumstances. In other words, as I see it, the crime is absolute. That's why the court's decision strikes me as scandalous, as well as dangerous and irresponsible: false justice tinged with bad sociological considerations." The chances were good, he added, that, on release from prison, the guy would "start again." There was nothing here, in Philippe's view of the matter, that departed from my own.

This was only half of the story, however. He then insisted that "when it comes to interpreting the crime, things are totally different: this was the crime of a rural subproletarian, and as difficult as it is to admit, this guy is a victim, *our* victim." To the extent, he continued, that "we comply with a world in which such acts are possible," there is "an incommensurable Injustice for which we should feel responsible." He added, "I think Claire, in her way, was saying the same thing."

I balked at this entirely class-based perspective, given that violence against women is common to all social classes. I wasn't sure, either, about *Injustice* with a capital *I*. Presumably it pointed to the systemic kind. But since when was violence against women any less systemic than class oppression? And concerning "such acts," toward whom should we feel responsible, the male who, whatever his social class, perpetrates them, or his female victim?

Setting the letters aside, I sensed I was still missing something. It seemed to me that to speak of justice as Claire and Philippe did, you had to assume a principle of equality against which to measure the discrepancy between this principle and the actual conditions in which people lived. What's more, to feel a sense of responsibility for the less fortunate required not only an awareness of your own privilege, but sufficient imaginative capacity to put yourself in their place. So far so good. But to me, the question remained whether you could expect this of someone who, while not individually responsible for systemic injustice, had come close to paying for it with her life. Whether you could, or should, say to her—within hearing distance of her spouse—"You know, your assailant is a victim, too." Whether you have the capacity to imagine what that sounds like, and to recognize that perhaps the victim should not be called upon to put herself in the place of the assailant—or, for that matter, in the place of third persons whose adjudication of incommensurables lacks a sense of timing.

In her last letter, Claire had remarked: "Maybe now isn't the time to say all this." Indeed. She had also stated, in the course of explaining her commitment to social justice, and addressing herself directly to Susan: "But you don't have to think about that side of things. You're a victim, that's the reality of your position, the one in which you have to save yourself, save both of you." But what had she asked Susan to do, and what had Philippe asked me to do, if not to think about "that side of things" as they saw it? Would I ever be able to do this? Had the time finally come? Or was it a matter, not of agreeing with them, but simply of understanding the position they themselves had been in?

What I could do now—now that I was no longer a mediator, now that I was largely healed and free of anger—was, at least, to try putting myself in their shoes. I could try to imagine, for example, how hard it must have been for Claire to be approached by this elderly, destitute couple, who had practically begged her for help. I could ask, in fairness to her, whether I myself could have turned them away, or whether I would have felt any better if, out of loyalty to us, she had done so. For that matter, I might attempt to picture how it would feel if a guest of ours had gone for a walk and been raped and almost murdered—or even, thinking of the couple, how it would feel if our own son had committed such an atrocious crime. And I could certainly appreciate the efforts Claire and Philippe had devoted to explaining themselves, even if those efforts had failed to produce the desired effect.

It's difficult to convey the results of these mental experiments. Although wary of believing it was possible to put myself in Claire and Philippe's place, I could see that time had loosened the defensive entrenchment in which I'd spent so many years of the aftermath, freeing me to go some distance in their direction. And I no longer detected even a trace of my former judgmental attitude. I'd changed. By the same token, the sense of having been betrayed by their failure to imagine the radically altered world in which we lived was no less acute, converting my newfound sympathy into something strangely abstract and suggesting that the conflict I was revisiting had simply lost its life in the wash of time, or that time itself had opened a chasm in its very passage. It was as if I were now reading about the demise of our friendship in a novel, with the detachment required to consider whether the characters' misfortune might be due not so much to individual shortcomings or cultural misunderstandings as to their relative positions in the wake of this seismic event, to a dissymmetry so profound that nothing could have served to bridge it. The whole thing became objectified, pointing to a damage no one could control, to a contingent and irredeemable loss inflicted by trauma.

I suppose I could have found some consolation in this. After all, if nothing could have prevented the loss, then perhaps there was no reason to regret it. Yet I was also reluctant to let go, to put these letters away among other personal effects to be discarded when I was gone. My thoughts about Philippe and Claire tasted of mortality, and not only of theirs.

The kitchen conversation with Susan—the one in which she said she was sorry for what I'd been through, including the loss of my friendship with Philippe and Claire—raised another issue. Thinking about the story I wished to tell of our experience, she suggested we go back to France and talk to her assailant. My jaw dropped. Why would we do that? To learn what was going through his mind as he raped and tried to kill her? Did we—or did I—care? Should I? Would he even know? Or have the verbal means to explain? And hadn't we gathered quite enough about him from the depositions, the psychiatric evaluations, the trial? I didn't see what purpose it could serve. Above all, I couldn't fathom why Susan would want to have anything further to do with this guy. "If you think it's such a good idea," I protested, "why don't *you* go talk to him?" "Well," she replied, "your French is better." My French! The language he'd almost ruined for me, with what she had called his "gestapo-like voice."

This exchange served to caution me against the tendency to assume that Susan and I always thought along the same lines on the subject of sexual assault. Yet wasn't that true? At least most of the time? And if so, what was I to make of this particular disagreement? Why had her suggestion met with an instantaneous and unyielding refusal on my part? I had no second thoughts about it. I had them, instead, about why that was the case.

My immediate response had felt like a physical clenching, a defensive reaction to some external stimulus. I recalled having found, on Google Earth, a satellite view of St.-Geoirs, then zooming in so close I could see the road Susan had walked down and, next to it, the tree-covered ravine in which the assailant had tried repeatedly to kill her. Not for a second did I forget that I was looking at a photograph—and yet the photograph alone was enough to set my heart racing and convince me that St.-Geoirs was forever off limits. Of course, if a meeting was arranged with the assailant, it would certainly not happen at the site of the crime and probably not anywhere near it. All the same: wouldn't I have to sit in his physical presence, look at his face and body, hear his voice?

But this was just as true for Susan as for me. So why had she been moved to propose the idea, while it would have been out of the question for me to do so? For one thing, I thought, she was the victim and had every right to make such a suggestion. The suggestion itself made sense when I considered that her anger had always been directed less at her assailant than at the culture that encouraged his crime and that had to be understood if it was to be fought. On the other hand, not only was I not the victim, but I still felt (and feel) complicit in that culture—and this, paradoxically, made me more rather than less resistant to meeting with the man. For even if understanding isn't the same as forgiving, how could I listen to him without making the imaginative effort to put myself "in his place"?

Maybe this is enough to explain my adamant refusal. There was something else, though, which had to do with recovery. In this, Susan had always been far ahead of me. She had to be. She had to take her recovery in hand right away in order to remake a self while grieving the one she'd lost in that ravine. In my own strange secondariness, I'd never quite known if I had a self to grieve—at least until the kitchen conversation. Now I know that my refusal to meet with her assailant also arose from loyalty to the young man I'd once been, the one who'd disappeared on that distant July 4th, and whose memory I would not betray.

The theme of second thoughts nevertheless entailed questions extending well beyond my attitude toward the assailant or toward Claire and Philippe. Had I been unfair to other people? People whose responses to Susan's plight or to my own had struck me as insensitive or ignorant? Had I been too hard on her parents, for example? Or even on the philosopher? At the same time, had I failed to fully appreciate those who had helped us? What I had a nagging need to understand above all was why the many examples of support didn't figure as prominently as I thought they should in my memory, or at least in my storytelling, while center stage was occupied disproportionately by instances of harm.

In boxes I hadn't opened in years I found countless letters and cards, almost all referring to the attack or its aftermath, commending us for our perseverance or responding to things we had said publicly. My mother wrote every week. My brothers, Jim and Gary, wrote as well. My niece Laura. My friend Alain. My colleagues Suzanne and Lionel. Many others. At times I was astonished by the insightfulness of the comments, contrasting so starkly with the clueless reactions we had suffered, especially in the early months. Yet all of these missives had been overshadowed, it seemed to me, by a far smaller number of hurtful encounters.

In this connection, I remembered discovering in the hospital that a single display of insensitivity could outweigh, in its effect, the abundant support we received. No doubt this striking imbalance reflected the upheaval of the event itself, which lent to normally negligible incidences—a thoughtless remark, an inconsiderate act, a dismissive look or attitude—the capacity to confirm that the world was indeed an untrustworthy place. And this symptom persisted for many months thereafter, if not longer. So was it any wonder that my memory appeared askew?

But I detected another disproportion, or another way of looking at the same one, more "economic" in character, and which I tested out in my own case. For if I thought of my traumatized self as a self whose reserves were seriously depleted, it seemed to go without saying that this self would have had to rely almost entirely on other people for replenishment. There would have been a substantial discrepancy between taking and giving, until my depleted self had regained the resources necessary to give and take in equal measure, or even give more than take. In the meantime, it may well be that the people who supported me, or us, didn't receive enough credit because I simply didn't have it to give. And to a person—me—already destitute, any threat requiring further expenditure for protection could have appeared unaffordable, and blown the threat itself out of all proportion.

The notion of a depleted self got me thinking again about the experience of invisibility. I had already learned about the role played in it by certain social or cultural attitudes—by a pervasive commonsense individualism according to which something had happened to Susan but not to Tom, or by the no less pervasive assumption that men aren't caregivers. But I hadn't yet reexamined the feeling I used to have of being marginalized in Susan's own storytelling or in the minds of her other listeners or readers.

The issue—the issue of my being recognized or not—came up instructively enough with the publication of *Aftermath*. So long after the assault, my reaction surprised not just Susan but me too, since I had read every page of the manuscript and didn't recall finding anything amiss as far as our relationship was concerned. I thought it would be a great book, which it was, and is. Yet when it appeared in print, and even more when the reviews started coming in, I felt unappreciated. I was touched by the dedication to Gabriel and me. And I knew I'd been mentioned numerous times in the narrative. Among these, however, my attention was drawn above all to this: "How could Tom go on teaching his classes, seeing students, chatting with colleagues . . . and why should he be able to walk down the street when I couldn't?"[2] The first part struck me as unfair. How could it fail to give the impression that I'd just gone on with my life while she lay at home, devastated? The fact was that teaching my classes and seeing students, carrying on in the world just two months after she'd narrowly escaped death—this was one of the hardest things I'd ever done. Which, moreover, I'd done for both of us. And then to suggest in addition that I was in the habit of "chatting" with colleagues, when in fact I was lying, exhausted, on the floor of my office . . .

The hurt of feeling unappreciated was compounded by the reviews. They discussed both the narrative and the philosophical components of Susan's book, not least the feminist view that the self is constituted through its relations with other selves. I was in complete agreement with this view, which I found all the more valuable as it tied the concept of the self to the empirical world, to real life, to the concrete experience of individuals. Yet as I remember, none of the reviews made more than a passing reference to the author's spouse, if they mentioned him at all. As if relationality stopped there.

But the reviews would never have upset me so much if I hadn't already felt neglected or misunderstood in the book, and I would not have felt as I did about the book unless, to begin with, as a caregiver and a person traumatized in his own right, I wasn't yearning for recognition. This, at any rate, may help to explain why, despite being a professor of literature, I'd somehow managed to disregard the *kind* of book Susan had written, a combination of story and essay designed to demonstrate the uses of personal narrative for philosophical reflection rather than to provide a full account of her experience, including my role in it. For that matter, how else could I understand my having made the same mistake as the reviewer who had criticized Susan for leaving her earlier chapters in their original form, where, among other things, there was so much anger? Couldn't I see that the reference to my "chatting with colleagues" was a reflection of that anger and not a criticism of me? Hadn't she made it clear enough? Only a few sentences before, she had stated: "The anger was still there, but it got directed toward safer targets: my family and closest friends."[3] On second thought, then, I'm convinced that my reading was largely selfish, not so much from a moral as from a clinical standpoint—which is not to offer excuses but simply to convey my sense that, in a post-traumatic context, vulnerability can give rise to a selfishness that's unaware of itself as such.

The issue of recognition never failed to come up in my effort to make sense of secondary trauma with the many therapists I saw over the years. The effort started with simply "doing therapy": arranging a first appointment with Melissa, getting in the car and driving to her place, opening up to her about the initial and ongoing awfulness, discussing fees and insurance, setting up a regular schedule and keeping to it. All of this could be said to reflect a recognition on my part that I was suffering from a condition I needed help with. Yet the recognition lay, really, in *doing* something about it. No doubt I was just beginning to appreciate that, in the wake of trauma, you don't just look for sense—you have to make it.

And you can only make it with other people. It was through my interaction with therapists that I achieved some understanding of what I'd call Major Spectral Disorder, a state of invisibility, inaudibility, and irreality familiar to all those prone to secondary trauma, including the numberless individuals whose spouses or partners have been seriously violated. Needless to say, MSD doesn't preclude additional diagnoses.

But I've also wondered at times if my reliance on individual psychotherapy alone didn't point to a lack of other resources, or else to my failure to look for them. Due to our itinerant lifestyle as well as the rudimentary public awareness of gender-based sexual violence in the 1990s, I probably never stopped to consider whether there might be, nearby, a group I could join. Yet I knew about Susan's experience with the rape survivors' group in Philadelphia. As she puts it in *Aftermath*:

> Hearing *other* survivors' *actual* narratives, in the context of group therapy, can also be healing, in ways that go beyond the capacity of individual therapy. It can not only enable a survivor to feel empathy for her traumatized self (by first feeling it for another who experienced a similar trauma), but also make possible appropriate emotions, such as anger, that she was not able to feel on her own behalf. By first feeling empathy with other survivors and getting angry with *their* tormentors, she is better able to get angry with her own. Hearing others' narratives can also help trauma survivors to move beyond unjustified self-blame. (Well, if *she* clearly wasn't to blame for her assault, why should I blame myself for mine?)[4]

I could imagine a men's group (heterosexual, in this case) in which a member voices his sense of failure: it seems he should have prevented his wife's or girlfriend's assault, or at least been able to fix things after it. The faces of the other men evince an intuitive recognition. They know the feeling. But one of them breaks in: "Look, there was no way you could have stopped this from happening. And since when is it your job to make it all better? Are you a superhero or something?" I could also imagine how this second guy might have said the same thing to himself more than once. Or even heard it from his therapist to begin with. But it hadn't stuck. Only when he hears the first guy does he become worthy of compassion in his own eyes. And then a third member of the group speaks up, with the odd impression of addressing *himself*: "You know, maybe your wife's needs wouldn't seem so overwhelming if you just quit blaming yourself. Maybe that's what she needs from you most of all."

I'm tempted to say I missed that boat, except that I don't really believe there was a boat to miss, a group I could have joined back then. But if there had been, would I have joined it? The evangelical milieu in which I'd grown up had made me suspicious of groups, especially those requiring the public display of private matters (as in witnessing to your salvation by the blood of Jesus, so as to encourage others along the same path or draw stray sheep back to the fold). And as it happened, my wariness of such intimacy jibed very well with certain widespread individualistic assumptions about masculinity that I, too, carried within me. Although Susan's assault and its aftermath had unsettled these assumptions, it took time for my behavior to catch up with what the upheaval suggested: for example, that male stoicism might be a weakness rather than a strength, not a resilience in the face of adversity but a resistance to facing it. Or that taciturnity, far from manifesting manly self-containment, could indicate the inarticulateness of one who is both opaque to himself and unattuned to others. It also took time to understand that the notion of masculinity supported by these assumptions was equipped with the means of its own enforcement: should you prove somehow inadequate to the notion—unable to control your environment, powerless to protect your loved ones, at a loss as to how to get on in life without help—you had only yourself to blame (or others, in the event that self-blame became intolerable, this being a major source of male violence). And this was to say nothing of the fact that you could be exposed to the scrutiny of your fellows, at the risk of being expelled from the club with no reimbursement of dues. It took time to realize how these symptoms of cultural pathology could have prevented me from talking to other men.

Meanwhile, I was writing. I mentioned earlier how my Holocaust book project, drawing on studies that predated the attack, allowed me to retrieve a sense of self in some measure independent of the attack and its aftermath, and also to find a way of talking about trauma by displacing the focus from sexual violence. It may sound simplistic, but not yet ready to speak, as a man, about violence against women, I'd chosen to speak as a Gentile about the horror inflicted on the Jews. The trouble, as I'd anticipated, lay in retooling: to understand how Holocaust survivors had tried to convey their ordeal required understanding the background provided by a body of work—in history, political science, psychology, philosophy, literature, film—that's essentially endless. And after years of reading, I had to go back, if better informed, to study the survivors' testimony. To do this, of course, I needed to rely on scholars who'd preceded me, and to many of whom I remain deeply indebted. Yet it was at this stage of my research that certain interpretations of Holocaust survivor testimony struck me as tendentious or even unresponsive, leaving survivors themselves, in my view, unlistened to. As if my post-traumatic antennae were suddenly on alert, I recalled how, in listening to Susan's many other listeners, I'd often been left with a similar impression. This—to abbreviate—may well explain why a basic issue among others came to occupy the central position in my book: in *Witnessing Witnessing*, I put myself in the place of a third person, watching, listening to, reading not only testimony but responses to it.

But things are never so simple. For where exactly was I—personally—in this triangular configuration? Why was it that, among the interpretations I found wanting, I tended to single out the ones most closely related to the post-structuralist theory in which I myself had been trained? Had I imagined reconnecting with a former self only to discover that I didn't like him very much? What these interpretations had in common was the assumption that trauma is "unspeakable"—so radical a departure from life as we know it, such a severe violation of human norms and expectations, that it cannot be expressed in words. And yet the survivors had found words. Words that, often by their own admission, may have seemed inadequate or insufficient, but with which nevertheless they had tried courageously to rejoin a community of speech after having been brutally silenced. I grew impatient with theoretical work so reliant on the tenuous assumption of "unspeakability" as to reinforce, if unintentionally, the silencing of the very survivors whose experience it claimed to represent. No doubt I also drew some satisfaction from being able, thanks to my long acquaintance with this work, to expose the operations of what struck me more and more as an ossified avatar. I know that some readers of *Witnessing Witnessing* have found that the book has an edge to it, and they may be right. I'm also willing to admit that the edge may owe something to my own experience of not having been listened to. But the anger and indignation I felt on behalf of Holocaust survivors was genuine, and for that I make no apology.

Perhaps this will give some idea of how the work of scholars can be informed by personal considerations even as we make every effort to produce scholarship worthy of the name. That said, during the many years in which I toiled away on the Holocaust book, I knew very well that another book was there, in abeyance. At times I could see something between or behind the lines I was typing, something like a watermark, a ghostly finger pointing beyond the pages as if to say, "By the way, when you're done with this . . ."

But when the time came, I wasn't so sure. What would be the point of revisiting all that pain? Susan had survived. She had rebuilt her life and was thriving professionally. Our marriage had weathered the upheaval. We had a son we loved (and who loved us back), secure jobs, a home. There were stresses and strains, and we'd lost several family members. Yet we'd come a long way. Why go back? And what if telling or retelling the story, and sharing my account with her, ended up reviving conflicts we assumed were behind us? I could think of nothing more regrettable than to jeopardize our relationship in the interest of a book whose purpose I couldn't even pin down.

Besides, I was bound to run into the challenges that confront any would-be memoirist, beginning with the fallibility of memory. True, I had a big box labeled *Grenoble* bursting with detailed documents of every imaginable stripe, which would help me wend my way through the early years without too much fear of betraying the historical facts. But how could I avoid the pitfall of misremembering or simply forgetting the unrecorded things? How could I be sure, at the same time, that I wasn't inventing things for the sake of the story? And how could I make sense of what had happened to Susan and me without conceding that it made sense?

I couldn't say for sure if these questions amounted to second thoughts, or simple misgivings, or excuses for not getting down to work. Or maybe newfound pretexts to silence myself in anticipation of imagined objections, such as that the story was Susan's and not mine (on the assumption that it couldn't be both) or that it was unseemly or politically objectionable for a man to talk about the effects on him of a suffering that men inflict on women. Without Susan's encouragement and support, I would have given up. On one occasion, she even convinced me to speak publicly about the attack, for the first time in twenty years.

The twentieth anniversary of the attack was also the last day of the Interplay Jazz Camp, run by friends of ours in Woodstock, Vermont. Susan was part of this musical community, which used the space in the Unitarian church during the week and had now gathered, with the Unitarians, for a Sunday morning service. On the drive to Woodstock, the sun shone over a quilt of open fields and forested hills not unlike the patchwork I'd observed while waiting, on that dirt road in St.-Geoirs, for Susan to return from her walk. As then, too, I was nervous, though for a different reason: knowing I'd felt silenced and that there would come a moment in the meeting when anyone could share news or concerns or thoughts, Susan had suggested that I stand and speak. I had run through all of the pros and cons, including my aversion to in-person "witnessing" (in a church, no less!), but couldn't make up my mind. At the very last second, as if tossing the dice, I rose from the pew and observed that on a fine summer day like today, exactly twenty years ago, Susan had gone for a walk and found herself ambushed, sexually assaulted, strangled, and left for dead at the bottom of a ravine. From the audience came a gasp, then a hush. I praised Susan for fighting back, adding that I was proud we had stayed together and remade our lives. I thanked everybody for giving us a sense of community. As I sat back down I couldn't avoid the impression of having committed an enormous gaffe.

Squirming in the pew, I waited for the meeting to run its course. I would have paid good money for an invisibility cloak beneath which I could have snuck out the door and texted Susan where to find me, most likely in the trunk of our car. As the gathering finally broke up, my escape was foiled by a woman who was curious to know where the attack had taken place. When I told her it had happened in France, she nodded and replied: "So, not here." In earlier years, such a remark would have rubbed me the wrong way. How many times had we heard this refrain, "not here," from people seeking reasssurance that horrific violence wasn't, couldn't be, a part of *their* world? But this time, as the woman left, I just smiled, seeing in her reaction less a manifestation of insensitivity to our story than an expression of vulnerability in those who listened to it. Meanwhile, Susan had been speaking to another member of the congregation. As we exited the church, she mentioned that the woman had approached her to say how sorry she was about the assault. But when Susan, having thanked the woman for her concern, added that "today is about Tom, my husband," there was no response. This, too, in years gone by, I might have found off-putting. But not now. My first impulse was to imagine that the story of Susan's assault had perhaps revived a deep pain in the woman's own past. Something had shifted inside me, bringing me closer to others by distancing me from myself.

We emerged at last onto the sidewalk, turned in the direction of our parking place, and hadn't taken ten steps when yet another woman, about to get into her car, stopped us and thanked me for speaking. Thanked me! I thanked her in turn. She thanked us both. We thanked her back. Much more and this exchange would have sounded like a Beckett play. As Susan and I made our way along the Woodstock green, hand in hand, I felt a strange lightness in my step, not just a metaphorical lightness, like psychological uplift, but a real physical elevation, as if someone had loosened a pressure valve. At the informal lunch later on, the leader of the congregation (who, in my memory, bore a remarkable resemblance to Liam Neeson) drew me aside and asked at length about my experience. I couldn't quite believe we were having this conversation, accustomed as I was to indifference or obliviousness. But a greater surprise lay in the discovery that, while talking with him, I felt no need for recognition, perhaps because he'd already granted it. My focus shifted to the nature of the experience itself—the experience of secondary trauma—which was far from mine alone and with which I suspect this man was already familiar, if not in his own life, then in what he may have learned about individual members of his church. Just getting the subject out there, between us, where he and I could both examine it, puzzle over it, even shake our heads together, converted it from the stuff of personal grievance to a condition that really mattered because so many people shared it. No longer a plaintiff, I felt almost like an emissary.

What I retained most of all from this occasion was the unforeseeability, the unscriptedness. Without the two women in the church, I would not have discovered myself so readily capable of compassion where anger had been the rule. Without the woman who thanked me, I would have continued to assume it was better to keep my mouth shut. Without the pastor, it would not have sunk in that to open my mouth was to put my story in its proper place, as just one among countless others that could be heard or read or imagined. I had always wanted to bear public witness to Susan's experience because of the very place from which I could do it. And not only at a Take Back the Night march or a community gathering such as this. But I also thought that, if I decided to write, it would be in the hope that people who found themselves in a position like mine would feel less alone in their solitude.

At the same time it seemed to follow from the very notion of unscripting that it might happen more than once. And it did. It led back to something Susan and I had shared from the moment we met, something we then appeared to have lost forever only to rediscover it, long after the attack, in an unexpected future. It led back to France.

15 *France*

The mere mention of Susan's assailant, as in our kitchen conversation, always recalled the difficulty I'd had in speaking and listening to French when I returned to my job after the attack. The language became tainted, right down to the physical acts required to produce it. I can't say how long this lasted. Even in the early days, to judge by the scrupulous crafting of my letters to Susan's lawyer or to Claire and Philippe, I cared as much about French as ever. Maybe it had to do with the difference between the spoken and the written word: as charged as the subject matter of the correspondence could be, the writing itself afforded me a measure of detachment, whereas the immediacy of speaking and listening could occasion what felt like sensorial proximity to the scene of the crime.

Be that as it may, the affliction eventually subsided. At a price. For somewhere in my unconscious, or subconscious, or preconscious—somewhere in the basement of my being—an accommodation was reached, allowing me to maintain the semblance of my former love while the genuine article languished in reserve. At least, this is how I understood things like my neglect to keep up with French culture and politics; my hesitation to communicate in French, despite the daily opportunity to do so and even long after the allergy had released me from its grip; and a disinclination to travel to France, which would previously have been unthinkable. These were symptoms of what is called, in Freudian terminology, decathexis: my passion had been withdrawn, with no immediate plan for reinvestment.

And if, indeed, I looked at myself as a case study, I failed to see how the withdrawal could be remedied. What had begun long ago as a fortuitous fondness for French in middle school and high school had led to my working at the kitchen table with Philippe on that July morning. It had proceeded through the required stages of college, graduate school, and an assistant professorship, all of which, despite the hard times, fit well enough together to make of those twenty-odd years a reasonably gratifying itinerary. Yet I'd gone into French because I loved it, not because I expected it to lead to a job. And now fate, if that's the word, had revealed a robust sense of irony. So enamored of French for opening the door to a different world, I found myself, at the arrival of the ambulance, facing that world in the form of a nightmare.

For sure, I could ask myself how big a deal the change could have been, given that, thirty years later, I was still a French professor. But the attack had placed me at a persistent and ghostly remove from my former professional self, at a distance both inescapable and so elusive that I could only apprehend it metaphorically: it was as if the professor had stayed on a train from which I'd disembarked, seeing no further point to the journey and leaving the professor, less and less certain of his own integrity, just hoping the other passengers wouldn't see through him. Then again, there were fleeting moments of dissociation in which the interval between these two selves could make itself felt without the aid of metaphors: the professor would be teaching a class or speaking in a formal exercise before colleagues when, *physically*, he sensed me hovering over his shoulder and whispering, Who do you think you are? There were even dreamlike moments when the professor, finding himself in some public place like a hotel lobby, would notice people casting quizzical glances in his direction and look down to discover a card pinned to his lapel, bearing not only his name but the counterfeit title Professor of French. At times, it really felt like I was working undercover, with false papers. Trained for so long to respect the truth, I even worried about my obituary, which would likely feature an official profile at the very moment when I'd no longer be in a position to set the record straight.

There were exceptions to this estrangement, occasions on which the status quo was disrupted and my young love of France appeared to revive, moments all the more uplifting as I could share them with Susan and Gabriel. Many years after the attack, Marie-Victoire, so supportive during and after the trial, invited us to stay at her family's property in Gordes, in the Vaucluse (Provence). There was an ancient stone house bordered by a huge hedge of fragrant rosemary; an olive press, no longer operating but structurally intact, with a millstone so massive it defied any attempt to imagine how it got there; the vestige of an outdoor bath, a good ten yards square, carved into the base of a shaded knoll, its knee-deep water perfectly clear and so cold, during our spring visit, that Gabe and I could barely walk across the basin before losing all sensation in our feet—a bath constructed, if not by the Romans themselves, at least during the time when they still ruled Gaul; and strange stone huts called *bories*, built without mortar and dating from the Bronze Age.

One afternoon, at loose ends, I wandered into a corner of the living room and peeked through the door of a tall wooden closet, empty except for a few papers strewn here and there. Out of idle curiosity, I picked up what looked like a pamphlet. On closer inspection, I could see it was actually an offprint. And then, astonished, I saw it was inscribed in the most personal terms to Marie-Victoire's parents by René Char, one of France's greatest twentieth-century poets and a major figure in the underground struggle against Nazism. "Oh yes," Marie-Victoire said to me, casually, accustomed as she was to the family lore, or distracted by the rosemary she was chopping as I burst into the kitchen, "they worked closely together in the Resistance." I wondered aloud if they'd also known Samuel Beckett, who had narrowly escaped the Gestapo in Paris and found refuge in the nearby village of Roussillon, where he was in contact with the *Maquis* (and where Gabriel, running up and down hills with other kids, rubbed into his clothes so much of the ochre-pigmented clay from which the village gets its name that, despite my laundering expertise, I never managed to wash it out). She wasn't sure about this, but she pointed out that right where we were standing, her parents had come within a hair's breadth of being arrested by the *Milice*, the fascist militia. And she mentioned that her mother had left a twenty-page account of their lives at the time, which I eagerly offered to translate for publication.

Nothing came of this, however. Marie-Victoire decided to leave her mother's text in the family archive, and I looked no further into the local history of the Resistance or even into Char's poetry. And although, on this trip and a few others we took to Paris in those years, I could still appreciate the many pleasures that had endeared me to France, there was never a moment at which those pleasures led me to revisit the idea, which I had once taken very seriously, of moving there. Of course, the idea had become idle for practical reasons, since our lives were so firmly anchored in the United States. Where would Susan and I find jobs? How would we even begin to build a community? And how could we uproot Gabriel from school—or from baseball? But while these considerations were decisive, I also noticed something missing: my former urge to get back to France as soon as I had left it. At the end of my graduate year in Strasbourg, where I studied with Philippe and Jean-Luc, I had an opportunity to stay on as a teacher of English in a secondary school and to complete an advanced degree in philosophy at the university. I declined, since, as an American, I had no future in the French university system. Yet I did so only after promising myself to return as soon as possible and for as long as I could manage. Ever since my earlier students days in Paris, I'd become miserable without a frequent fix of France. Now, the road back was barred, emotionally and psychologically, offering at most a telescopic view of bygone days, a residual recognition of the kind you'd expect at the twenty-fifth reunion of your high school graduating class.

I might have remained forever in this limbo if I hadn't drifted toward the French Caribbean. In my courses on twentieth-century French narrative prose, I felt the urge to branch out from the metropolitan canon (Proust, Gide, Camus, Sartre, Duras, Robbe-Grillet, Sarraute, and others) and was really taken with Antillean writers, especially the Guadeloupean Maryse Condé and the Martinican Patrick Chamoiseau. It wasn't just a matter of the literary merit of their work, which was obvious. What appealed to me as well was the complexity of their position: both were consummate wordsmiths, wielding French to impressive effect, and both knew the white Western literary canon from the inside, often adapting it to their own purposes; but both wrote from outside the white mainstream, with a deep appreciation for Antillean culture and an acute awareness of the history of slavery and colonialism.

Maybe, too, I felt drawn to these writers because I was already so immersed in the testimony of Holocaust survivors. The impulse that had led me, by way of trauma studies, to take a consuming interest in what these survivors had suffered was opening the door to another order of suffering in another part of the world. And yet here, everything went through French.

Not that this literature—or Susan's and my acquaintance with Condé, or our later friendship with Chamoiseau, or the many trips we made to Guadeloupe and Martinique—entailed anything like a simple return to France. After all, there is no return to life before trauma. Yet the Antilles seemed to invite a renewed, if altered, relationship with what we had lost, most likely because they themselves are both French and not French. Although converted long ago from colonies into full-fledged departments analogous to states in the U.S., the islands differ from France not only in their geography and climate but in their history and demographics, the vast majority of inhabitants being people of color descended from Africans once enslaved by the French. And they live in a land of *diglossie*: while French is the official language, imposed by the government in Paris, everyone also knows Creole, derived largely from French and African languages in the era of slavery—and, at least until recent decades, broadly stigmatized. This inegalitarian bilingualism plays a central role in Chamoiseau's childhood memoirs, for instance, where the boy who spoke Creole at home and in the street found it strictly forbidden at school, even as instruction in the mandatory French could prove humiliating. True, the memoirs were written by a verbal virtuoso, attesting to how French became for him the indispensable medium in which to convey the weight of history borne by his family, his milieu, the islands themselves. But that's not the end of the story: in his work, as in that of many Antillean writers—and in keeping with the increasingly robust affirmation of the islands' distinctive culture—French is changed, from the inside, by Creole.

This is probably why the further I delved into French Caribbean literature, the more I grew to appreciate the doubleness—not just the *diglossie* but also the transformative potential of work written in French by Creole "outsiders." Although the Creole language is often found in quoted dialogue, its presence can be discerned as well, for example, in vocabulary that's spelled the standard way but isn't French. I'd be reading along and stumble on *blogodo* or *ouélélé*, words I wouldn't find in a French dictionary but that, since I had to look for them elsewhere, would inevitably teach me something about Creole culture over and above their own definitions. These and many other expressions seemed to invigorate the French language, to promise new growth beyond its highly regulated orthodoxy. At the same time, in writing of a satirical nature, I detected a kind of literary jujitsu whereby the very tools of eloquence acquired by Antillean writers from their French education were enlisted in the resistance to cultural imperialism.

Just as telling for me was how this literature opened new perspectives on the geography of the islands, as in Édouard Glissant's oft-quoted remark, "Our landscape is its own monument."[1] Yes, you could look at the islands in exactly the way tourist agencies wanted you to, as white sand beaches overarched by majestic palm trees waving in the breeze, as beautiful Martinican women dancing the *biguine* or preparing to serve you a filet of the day's catch *au colombo*. But you could also look at a field of sugar cane or hike through a forest that would bring to mind the unspeakable barbarity of plantation life or the terror of escaped slaves, just as you could gaze at a lovely surf capable of conjuring the murderous ships that once sailed the Caribbean and added the bones of countless Africans to those white sands so prized by tourists. And this, in its way, raised an unavoidable question. It wasn't a matter of thinking I could never again enjoy the beauty of the islands because of what I'd learned about their history. After all, the Antilleans I knew appreciated that beauty. And they also appreciated the French language. Which is to say that I had to ask myself: If people descended from slaves, people who still suffered from discrimination, could live with and even thrive in French, and if the writers among them chose to deploy the language with such virtuosity—and if, finally, it was thanks to this language that I'd had the chance to get to know the writers and many others—then why should I think that French was a dead letter for me?

The stimulus of this new world proved indeed all the more decisive thanks to personal relationships. One day I contacted Patrick Chamoiseau to see if we could discuss the possibility of his visiting Princeton. We met at a café in Fort-de-France and started making plans (little knowing that COVID-19 would soon put everything on hold). A few days later, Patrick extended an invitation from friends of his to a dinner at their house. It turned out to be a celebration of our hosts' fiftieth wedding anniversary, attended by people—artists, actors, friends and family—all of whom knew each other but had never laid eyes on us. A celebration at which we were treated as guests of honor, welcomed with a hospitality so generous and even magical as to make me wonder if I was being duped by my own naïveté. At one point early in the evening, Patrick, having served us a ti' punch (agricultural rum with cane sugar and a lime wedge), gestured toward a woman just approaching and said, smiling, "C'est ma soeur. C'est la Baronne." *La Baronne!* His sister, "The Baroness," loomed very large in the memoirs I just mentioned. She was the eldest of five children in the Chamoiseau family and ran the show at home whenever their mother required a strong auxiliary. To me, *la Baronne* was a figure of literary, even mythical, grandeur, somebody I would never have imagined meeting in real life. It was as if Marcel Proust had just introduced me to the Duchesse de Guermantes. I bowed. I even stammered, "Mais Madame, vous êtes légendaire!" She just chuckled. Maybe she didn't know how famous Patrick had made her. Or didn't care. Later that evening, when people had finished eating and, mellowed by wine, were casually changing places around the table, I was talking with Ernest Brêleur, the artist (our host, with his spouse, Mimi), when I heard a familiar refrain: "Il y a longtemps que je t'aime / Jamais je ne t'oublierai" (I have loved you for a long time / Never will I forget you). I turned around and saw Susan and Mimi and The Baroness sitting together. They were singing "À la claire fontaine," the very song Susan had been singing, so many years before, as she set out on her walk in St.-Geoirs.

For practical reasons, Patrick's initial visit to Princeton was remote. Yet his discussions with faculty and students were so engaging as to suggest a longer, in-person arrangement, which we scheduled for the fall of 2024. The focus was on a seminar called "From Slavery to Globalization," whose success can be judged from a group photo taken on the last day of class, in which the graduate students, not always the merriest demographic (as I know, having been one of them) are smiling unrestrainedly. There were also any number of events, such as a conference I organized around Patrick's work and interests (and which included a jazz concert and a showing of the film *Biguine*, for which he wrote the script), as well as appearances in New York, Philadelphia, and Washington where I accompanied him and his spouse, Ghyslaine. Here again, the personal interactions mattered as much as anything—just traveling together, for example, or sharing the mundane concerns of everyday life. After class, when Patrick and I always went for a beer, we might still be talking about Aimé Césaire but just as often about gym passes or Westerns on TV. Things I'd long grown accustomed to thinking of as a chore or a nuisance I started looking forward to, like grocery shopping, which, with Patrick and Ghyslaine, became an outing, even a collaboration, as when it took all three of us to find the right ingredients for a Creole soup. On our excursions to a Macy's in one of those dreadful malls on Route 1 in search of winter clothing—an essential item for them as soon as the temperature in New Jersey dropped below seventy degrees—I surprised myself having fun. Through their eyes, even American suburban life in its numbing familiarity assumed an air of novelty, reminding me of how, when I first lived in France, even the billboards were stimulating. This and much more, in the daily contact over three months, often with Susan (who took us all to concerts), grew into a friendship I hadn't expected when I extended an institutional invitation to Patrick. Shortly after the semester ended, Patrick and Ghyslaine welcomed us to their family's Christmas Eve party in Martinique, which we didn't leave until 2:30 in the morning.

And our group of Martinican friends kept growing. Patrick put me in touch with Manuel, who teaches at the University of the Antilles and who, when asked if we might go for a hike on the *traces*, the trails that crisscross the island, enlisted two eminent botanists—one of them credited with the discovery of nine plant species, all bearing his name in Latin—for a guided introduction to the rainforest. Manuel has driven us around Schoelcher and Fort-de-France on jaunts as thrilling as any amusement ride I've ever been on, and with his partner, Sylvie, has regaled us with Creole cuisine, agricultural rum, and numberless stories about Martinique. I don't recall having ever left their house without the gift of a book from Manuel's collection, be it an out-of-print study of French Antillean culture, a volume of *biguine* piano scores for Susan, an illustrated survey of Caribbean fruit trees, or an encyclopedic dictionary of Martinican fishing (from which I've learned that the same fish can go by half a dozen names in as many villages, further stimulating my interest in Creole while eliminating any hope of mastering it). Manuel, in turn, put me in touch with Robert, who had trained teachers of Creole for decades. Despite being a slow student, I proudly call Robert *mon prof de Créole*. One day, at my request, he gave us a tour of Fort-de-France, offering commentary on its many neighborhoods, including Volga Plage, where a run-down residential area lies next to the bay and its container terminal, at once a technological marvel and a reminder of the island's debilitating dependency on imports—and also Texaco, which I'd really wanted to see, the subject of *Texaco,* Patrick's prize-winning novel. We later climbed to Balata, where Susan and I learned more about Martinique's extraordinary trees and Robert showed us how to harvest almonds. And then there's our oldest friend, Béatrice, who welcomes us back every year with a smile whose warmth and generosity we can feel before we've even landed at the airport.

As I said, everything here—not just my research but, more important, these friendships—goes through French. So much so, and for long enough now, that I have the sense of being *in* the language again. Or of having it in me. I don't recoil when I hear it, which sometimes happened in the first years after Susan's attack. I don't have to mourn its loss, either, as I did later on, like an amputee suffering phantom pain. And on speaking it, I don't feel like I'm betraying Susan or myself. Which is to say that the Caribbean has not only brought us back, in a way, to France and to each other at a new, if different, beginning; it has also reminded me that it's okay, after trauma—it's permissible, it's all right, you're allowed—to experience pleasure once again.

In the fall of 2024—during the very semester when Patrick was visiting Princeton and when he and I and Susan and Ghyslaine spent so much time together—there took place, in Avignon, France, the now famous Pelicot trial. Police had discovered that, over a period of more than nine years, Dominique Pelicot had not only drugged and raped his wife, Gisèle, but invited many other men to rape her while he filmed and photographed them. Dominique and fifty others were brought to trial on charges of rape, attempted rape, and/or sexual assault and were all convicted, with varying sentences. Although the egregiousness of the crime, or crimes, was beyond dispute, the case would never have drawn such worldwide media attention had Gisèle not waived her right to anonymity and insisted on a public trial. Thanks to Gisèle's extraordinarily courageous political commitment, the systemic nature of sexual violence against women was fully exposed. In a trial with fifty-one defendants (although more perpetrators were involved, some remaining unidentified despite the videos and photos)—men differing in age, civil status, ethnicity, profession, and generally well regarded by their families and friends—no one could claim that rape was the act of a lone, aberrant, crazed, or monstrous individual. In a trial where the accused had bonded over images posted to the internet and where more than a few of them asserted that, in spite of all evidence to the contrary, Gisèle had consented to the act or else that the act was sufficiently justified by the consent of her husband, to suggest that no shared assumptions underlay male sexual aggression would obviously have begged the question. In a trial that showed for all to see that the legal definition of rape didn't even broach the matter of consent, it was impossible to deny the gender-based bias of the French criminal code. Thanks to Gisèle Pelicot, that code was subsequently amended, and hopes were raised that the trial would serve to alter the landscape of gender relations in France and perhaps elsewhere.[2] At the same time, those hopes are up against a deeply entrenched sexism. How optimistic one can afford to be when one considers that the very media enabling public awareness of the case are also responsible for a news cycle so brief as to have induced in the public a kind of attention deficit? And once the trial was over, once the curtain had gone down and the actors and spectators had dispersed, I couldn't help wondering about Gisèle, about her children, about the families of the convicted men and their communities, about all those people who had to get on with their lives. How did they cope?[3]

It was during the same period—the fall of 2024—that I discovered, thanks to a colleague, the book entitled *Sambre* and the TV series based on it.[4] Sambre is the name of a river in northern France, in the vicinity of which Dino Scala, "the rapist of the Sambre," committed the majority of his more than fifty sexual assaults between 1988 and 2018. He was arrested in 2020, tried and convicted in 2022, and sentenced to twenty years (the maximum for rape under French law). I was initially surprised, even a bit embarrassed, not to have known about this. I was even more surprised (and somewhat less embarrassed) to learn that most of my French friends hadn't heard about it either. But the greatest surprise of all came in reading the book, to which the author, Alice Gérard, had devoted painstaking research and a professional writer's flair, an account motivated by several questions: How did he get away with it—for thirty years? How was it possible that so few people knew about it? How do you explain an attention deficit having nothing to do with the digital age?

Those 450 pages tell, and retell, in reference to police and judicial authorities, a tale of indifference, insensitivity, or outright hostility to victims (all of them female, many in their teens), of legal and procedural inadequacy, administrative carelessness, jurisdictional disconnection, class discrimination, and more. They also describe Scala's "method," which helped him escape detection and which, aside from choosing a time and place unlikely to attract witnesses, included approaching the victim from behind, wrapping a cord around her neck to silence her, never allowing her to see his face, and most often leaving her unconscious from strangulation. We learn as well that like Dominique Pelicot and his collaborators, Scala was a "regular guy": a husband, a father, the captain of his local soccer team. At the same time, the author deftly individualizes and integrates the multitude of victims' stories and duly credits those public officials who, with the help of updated technology, facilitated the arrest and prosecution of the perpetrator. In sum, Gérard produced a remarkably comprehensive and compelling documentary narrative. And yet, while *Sambre* can be said to explain how Dino Scala raped with impunity for thirty years, thanks to its portrayal of the political culture that enabled him to do so, it still leaves you asking how this was possible.

The effect this book had on me was due in large part to there being, as in Susan's attack, a single rapist, and one who strangled his victims—a rapist on whom I could focus the full force of my repulsion. But in addition, what happened to the victims often evoked, in my imagination, what *could have happened* to Susan. For example: telling your story only to be met with disbelief or suspicion. Yet the TV series had an even greater impact, no doubt because of its visual immediacy. Thus, in the opening episode, Scala's first victim is forced, shortly after reporting her attack to the police, to participate in a *reconstitution*, or reenactment, returning to the scene of the crime and lying back down at the very spot where she had regained consciousness. Susan, while still in her hospital bed in Grenoble, had been informed of this investigative exercise by her newly hired lawyer and instantly refused to have anything to do with it. Seeing this on-screen just strengthened my conviction from long ago that it could only be retraumatizing for the victim. And then other parts of the episode recalled what *did* happen to Susan: the initial scene shows this same woman lying, bloodied and lacerated, on an isolated embankment by the Sambre; in a subsequent scene, she's told by police that, because she survived, she's "lucky"; and still later, at home during a dance party suggesting a return to normal life, she jumps, startled, when a guest standing at her back taps her on the shoulder, recalling a moment when, with no warning, a friend of Susan's, who knew about the attack, unthinkingly bear-hugged her from behind.

Watching this episode, I didn't need to take my pulse or reach for my blood pressure monitor to know how upsetting it was for me, to realize that after all these years I was still capable of intense emotional flashbacks, along with despair at the tenaciousness of sexual violence everywhere one looks. What I learned about the victims of the Sambre, what I learned from the Pelicot trial, might have turned me away from France right when I seemed to be heading back in that direction. But instead, the stories of these courageous women made me want more than ever to pursue the path I was already taking, made me want to understand much better, in the French Caribbean, the connections between racial injustice and gender oppression. One night, in Fort-de-France—again, in the fall of 2024—Patrick arranged for Susan to meet George Arnaud, a prominent feminist and political activist, past president of the Union des Femmes de Martinique. I went along, as did Patrick, Ghyslaine, and Manuel. Among other things, George was hoping that Susan might give a public lecture on her next trip to the island. I just listened, excited by this encounter and by all I had yet to learn.

In the spring of 2025, Susan delivered a keynote address in Toulouse at a conference on sexual violence. It was the first time she'd spoken French in such a public way since the trial of her assailant, and also, as it happened, an occasion for colleagues to express their appreciation of *Aftermath* in its French translation. From Toulouse, and during a trip to Paris a month later, she phoned me at home in Vermont. She sent photos and videos. We FaceTimed. The interaction with French colleagues, the street activity, the art exhibits, the outdoor markets—all of this made for an unmistakable happiness, even an exuberance, in her demeanor and her voice. More than once she said, "You should come with me next time!"

I agreed. Yet it still gave me pause. After all, I'd gone back quite a few times since the attack, and nothing had really changed until I'd turned toward Martinique and Guadeloupe, where the distance from France isn't measured only in kilometers. On the other hand, the matter depended mostly on language, and I'd never forgotten how our Antillean friends had made me feel at home again in French. So that now, I had to ask myself: If Susan, who was sexually assaulted and almost murdered in French, could feel happy once more in that language, then what was holding me back?

And then there was this: that while lives are always composed of concurrent narratives—narratives moving between foreground and background, joining or disjoining, off to one side or the other or hovering somewhere on the horizon—I'd learned the hard way that the story you tell yourself in order to make sense of a world that no longer makes it for you can eclipse all the others, and that you can come to rely on it so thoroughly as to end up being its prisoner. True, I'd been lucky to learn that this constraint isn't unbreakable, thanks to the new chapter opened for us by the arrival of Gabriel (now living, and thriving, in Los Angeles). And it was doubtless this chapter that had attuned me to the possibility of another new beginning, the one I detected on FaceTime, not so much in Susan's words as in her smile—a smile that said there was much more to our lives than a trauma narrative.

What struck me as well was that these forward-looking moments had the feel of a reminiscence. At one point I realized they were sending me back to that magical night in Martinique and the glow on Susan's face—I want to say her countenance—as she was singing. I wanted to tell her about this but by then it was late and she was sound asleep in France. So I just sang to her in my imagination:

Il y a longtemps que je t'aime
Jamais je ne t'oublierai

Acknowledgments

I would not even have begun this book without the encouragement of my spouse, Susan J. Brison. Along the way, I insisted that if at any moment it came between us, I'd drop it. But her support never wavered, nor did her willingness to read drafts or her permission to share publicly the story of so personal a trauma. I hope the book will reflect my gratitude for her generosity and my admiration of her courage in fighting gender-based violence.

Writing the book was also an occasion to revisit, with our son, Gabriel, many moments from his earlier years. As it turned out, "revisiting" wasn't just a return to what we already knew but a discovery of the past and of each other, for which I'm deeply grateful. I'm also lucky that, like his mother, Gabriel has a very keen editorial eye.

I owe thanks for quite a number of readings. At an early but crucial stage, Mark Johnson, Michael Levine, and Judith Sanders helped me remain true both to myself and to my imagined audience. Suzanne Nash read a later version of the manuscript with the compassion and insight I'd always appreciated in the years we worked together at Princeton. Most recently, Helen Benedict, Stéphane Gerson, and Leo Kittay offered invaluable commentary that allowed me, at last, to send the book off.

It would be impossible to mention all of the people who have supported us over the thirty-five years since Susan's assault. In addition to my family, thanks go especially to Marie-Victoire Louis and Monique Middleton, whose friendship included accompanying us to the trial of Susan's assailant and transcribing the entire proceedings. Thanks go as well to Eva and Jeffrey Kittay and Margot

Livesey, and to the many therapists who helped us, above all Melissa Bailey, Peter Collier, Ronald Green, Mark Johnson, and Gary Karpf. I am grateful to André Benhaïm, Chad Córdova, Danielle Tumminio Hansen, Sena Hill, Carolyn Jenks, Michael Jennings, Alice Kaplan, Daniel Lieberfeld, Dawn Skorczewski, and Charly Verstraet for their abiding interest in the project.

Heartfelt thanks to my editor, Naomi Schneider, who made this book happen, and who showed unfailing sensitivity toward an author faced with so fraught a subject. Also at the University of California Press, thanks to Aline Dolinh, Emily Grandstaff, Francisco Reinking, and Jolene Torr for their expert guidance. My gratitude goes as well to Jan Spauschus for dexterous copyediting, to Sophia Millman for timely research assistance, and to Cassie Mannes Murray for creative collaboration in publicity.

Finally, I am deeply indebted to our many dear friends in Vermont and Martinique. You know who you are.

Note to the Reader

The names of certain people referred to in this memoir have been changed.

Notes

4. The Assault

1. A colloquial translation of “il le faut” would be “I have to.” I leave “it’s necessary” in order to convey the chill of a phrase also used by the public prosecutor when exhorting Susan to forget the attack (see chapter 8).

7. Living On

1. Statistics pertaining to sexual assault vary widely and do not reflect the real number of incidences, given how often the crime remains unreported. See, among other sources: the 2024 National Crime Victimization Survey (https://bjs.ojp.gov/document/cv24.pdf), the National Intimate Partner and Sexual Violence Survey (https://www.cdc.gov/nisvs/media/pdfs/sexualviolence-brief.pdf), the FBI’s Crime Data Explorer (https://cde.ucr.cjis.gov/LATEST/webapp/#/pages/home), and the Rape, Abuse & Incest National Network (https://rainn.org/get-informed/facts-statistics-the-scope-of-the-problem/).

2. See, for example, the special issue of *Psychological Trauma: Theory, Research, Practice, and Policy* 15, no. S2 (2023), https://www.apa.org/pubs/journals/special/tra-secondary-trauma-pdf.

3. See the groundbreaking work by Helen Benedict, *The Lonely Soldier: The Private War of Women Serving in Iraq* (Beacon Press, 2009).

4. Susan Brison, *Aftermath: Violence and the Remaking of a Self* (Princeton University Press, 2002/2023), 120–21.

8. The Trial

1. This suspicion was confirmed most recently by the conduct of defense lawyers in the trial of Dominique Pelicot and fifty other men accused of sexual assault (see the last chapter of this memoir). Regarding the victim, Gisèle Pelicot, claims or suggestions were made about complicity in sexual play (https://www.francebleu.fr/infos/faits-divers-justice/proces-des-viols-de-mazan-gisele-pelicot-quitte-la-salle-alors-qu-une-avocate-interprete-ses-reactions-sur-une-video-2852890), exhibitionism (https://www.franceinfo.fr/faits-divers/affaire-des-viols-de-mazan/vous-n-auriez-pas-des-penchants-exhibitionnistes-au-proces-des-viols-de-mazan-gisele-pelicot-confrontee-aux-questions-inquisitrices-de-la-defense_6788512.html), and alcoholism (https://www.lepoint.fr/societe/proces-des-viols-de-mazan-j-ai-l-impression-d-etre-la-coupable-s-insurge-gisele-pelicot-18-09-2024-2570630_23.php).

9. And Now

1. Brison, *Aftermath*, 108–9.

11. More Trouble

1. William Ernest Henley, "Invictus" from *Poems* (Macmillan and Co., 1920), 83–84.
2. Primo Levi, *Survival in Auschwitz*, trans. Stuart Woolf (Macmillan, 1993), 152–53.

13. Untimeliness

1. Olga Tokarczuk, *Drive Your Plow Over the Bones of the Dead*, trans. Antonia Lloyd-Jones (Riverhead, 2018), 243–44.

14. Second Thoughts

1. Brison, *Aftermath*, xi–xii.
2. Brison, *Aftermath*, 14.

3. Brison, *Aftermath*, 13.

4. Brison, *Aftermath*, 73.

15. France

1. Édouard Glissant, *Caribbean Discourse: Selected Essays*, trans. J. Michael Dash (University Press of Virginia, 1989), 11.

2. Gisèle Pelicot, *A Hymn to Life: Shame Has to Change Sides*, trans. Natasha Lehrer and Ruth Diver (Penguin, 2026).

3. See Rachel Aviv's article "A Family Trial" in *The New Yorker*, March 2, 2026.

4. See Alice Gérard, *Sambre: Radioscopie d'un fait divers* (Éditions Jean-Claude Lattès, 2023).